THE PRICE GUIDE
TO
19th AND 20th CENTURY
BRITISH PORCELAIN

*by David Battie
and Michael Turner*

Published by THE ANTIQUE COLLECTORS' CLUB
Woodbridge,
Suffolk.

Printed by
Baron Publishing, Woodbridge, Suffolk.

To Sarah

Contents

Foreword

The Antique Collectors' Club

Club membership, which is open to all private collectors, costs £7.95 per annum. Members receive free of charge the Club's magazine (published every month except August), which contains well-illustrated articles dealing with the practical aspects of collecting not normally dealt with by magazines. Prices, features of value, investment potential, fakes and forgeries are all given prominence in the magazine.

In addition members buy and sell among themselves; the Club charges a nominal fee for introductions but takes no commission. Since the Club started nine years ago many thousands of antiques have been offered for sale privately. No other publication contains anything to match the long list of items for sale privately which appears monthly.

The presentation of useful information and the facility to buy and sell privately without the middle man's profit would alone have assured the success of the Club but perhaps the feature most valued by members is the ability to make contact with other collectors living nearby. Not only do members learn about other branches of collecting but they make interesting friendships.

As its motto implies, the Club is an amateur organisation designed to help private individuals get the most out of collecting; it is informal and friendly and gives enormous enjoyment to all concerned.

The Antique Collectors' Club

5 Church Street, Woodbridge,

Suffolk.

For Collectors – By Collectors – About Collecting

Acknowledgements

Our thanks are due to all the experts at Sotheby's Belgravia and Sotheby's Bond Street who have helped us with information. We are particularly grateful to Hugh Gibson of Royal Doulton and Minton, Henry Sandon of the Dyson Perrins Museum at Worcester, John Twitchett, Honorary Curator of the Royal Crown Derby Museum, Terence A. Lockett for his assistance with the Davenport items, Mr. Levy for his help on the Minton figures and to all the collectors and dealers who have supplied objects, comment or criticism and who wish to remain anonymous.

We are indebted to John and Diana Steel for their patience and understanding and to Jeanette Kinch for taking the vast majority of the photographs. Lastly thanks to Sarah Battie for typing some of the copy and for tolerating David's ill humour when he was typing it himself.

Descriptions of illustrations on the dust jacket are as follows:

Front Cover: Royal Worcester elephant flower holder after a model by James Hadley. Ivory-coloured body and brightly coloured and gilt details. 8¾in. 1877.

Spine: Wedgwood Fairyland "Candlemas" Vase with brightly coloured pixies, dragons and central figures formed from melting candles. 10¼in. 1920's.

Back Cover: Coalport vase and cover on blue céleste ground c.1861, probably painted by James Rouse.

Price Revision List

1st March annually

The usefulness of a book containing prices rapidly diminishes as market values change, for prices can fall as well as rise.

In order to keep the prices in this book fully up-dated a revised price list will be issued on 1st March each year. This list will contain the current values of all the pieces illustrated in the book.

To ensure that you receive the Price Revision List yearly, complete a banker's order form and send it to the Antique Collectors' Club now.

The Price Revision List costs £1.25 a year by banker's order or £1.50 cash, from:—

**THE ANTIQUE COLLECTORS' CLUB,
5 CHURCH STREET, WOODBRIDGE, SUFFOLK**

Important Note

This book is a price guide, and the estimates given reflect actual prices reached at a major London auction room, mainly within the last few months. Prices fluctuate all the time, on some objects or classes of objects quite wildly. The prices given here are for good examples in good condition, unless otherwise stated. A damaged or tired example could range from the lower estimate to zero, whereas a really superb example might double the upper limit. Obviously, if the book is being used to decide how much to spend on buying from a dealer, his profit must be added to the estimate given, probably thirty per cent of the upper limit.

Factors Which Influence Prices

Buyers

It is possible to divide the potential purchasers of any object into five categories, although there is some degree of overlapping. These are: The Collector, The Dealer, The Decorator, The Joker and, a relative newcomer, The Investor.

The Collector usually specialises in one factory or style and he, or others like him, have been collecting for years, establishing a scale of prices which is fairly predictable. It is possible, however, for something to spark off wider interest in the Collector's subject — an exhibition, a definitive book or a television programme — which will radically affect values. Usually the comparative values remain the same while the individual items increase by the same proportion. This upsets the established Collector who is grossly affronted by these new upstarts muscling in on his territory. His letters to the editor, and sometimes conversation as well, are padded with phrases like "I remember when" and "a few years ago" as he sees one particular subject thrown wide open to an expanding and expensive market. Many, unable to bear the strain, sell out, possibly to start on another, undefiled, field; others settle down secure in the knowledge that they have beaten the market. The Collector is more frequently found in shops than in auction rooms but the serious one does take auction catalogues and, if he wishes to bid for an object, will either do so by leaving the bid with the auctioneer or bidding through a dealer.

The Dealer more frequently than not has a shop and is often known for specialising in one type of object. He buys privately from the street markets, from other dealers, or from the auction rooms and, since he lives by selling his goods, knows fairly exactly the prices which he can afford to pay to allow himself a profit.

The Decorator can be a private buyer or, more often, a dealer who specialises in objects that will be sold more for use and display than for their origin. For example, the Royal Worcester violinist (p.102) is a rare and collectable piece but is more likely to be bought by the Decorator than the Collector.

These three groups can be beaten by the Joker. The Jokers are wild

— literally. Completely unpredictable, their one constant contribution is the introduction into the auction scene of either unlimited money or unlimited lack of understanding of the state of the market. The Joker may be a passer-by who takes a liking to a vase and feels he must own it. He may wish to decorate a room in his house in a particular style and will buy every piece at an inflated price until he is satisfied; the prices may then either drop or continue at the new scale as everyone has now mentally adjusted to them. He may be the collector of a particular subject, such as plates painted with horses, or teapot stands. It is the Joker element which makes quoting prices at auction so difficult and potentially inaccurate especially out of London — and it can also stretch to places. An auction held in a country town can result in prices that would send home empty-handed a London dealer who had gone hoping to buy. Since the vast majority of objects of quality are sold in the capital, a good country sale will have the local dealers and collectors falling over themselves. Conversely, a poorly attended sale on a wet day too far from London could be full of cheap lots.

It might be as well to dispel once and for all the myth that there is a good time and a bad time of year to sell. A London auction will attract dealers and collectors from all over the world at any time of year, ease of international travel and the shortage of top pieces contributing to this.

A fairly new cross-breed now making his presence felt in the market is The Investor — somewhere between The Collector, The Dealer and The Joker. The thoroughbred Investor (as opposed to the investor who rather likes antiques and invests his spare money with reasonable caution) is a newish breed. In the extreme case, he is convinced that antiques are a marvellous investment and proceeds to spend money on the area of the market which appeals to him. His cupidity is matched only by his laziness, with the result that, in this extreme case, he buys wildly without troubling to understand what he is buying, his sole criterion being what he considers a "good buy". Inherited from his horse-racing/Stock Exchange background is the habit of buying and selling quickly, with large sums at stake. He views antiques much as he does copper, gold, sugar, tin, stocks, shares or any other definable commodity. Individual quality is not considered. His eagerness for a "fast buck" results in his disposing of his investment too quickly and, as most of what he buys is of poor quality (i.e. his "good buys"), he loses money and thereafter condemns antiques and those who handle them in a loud voice. The silver crash of 1970/71 saw the death of some of the more colourful horses of this breed.

Damage

Porcelain loses a great deal of its value through damage which, however well restored, is always detectable. To a serious collector, forced to buy a damaged piece for lack of a better example, such a piece is a constant source of irritation, to be sold as soon as a better example — even at five times the price — comes along. A very rough guide is that slight damage — a hair crack, chip or rim or finger or knop restored — will destroy up to two-thirds of the value of the object, worn gilding or flaked enamel can reduce it by half. A smashed piece, unless of large size and usable, such as a jardinière, has practically no value. On the other hand, a top class piece in immaculate condition could command double the upper limits given in the guide.

It is worth remembering that there is almost no investment value in a damaged piece. If one resells after a number of years, one is likely to lose money, whereas in reselling a perfect piece one is likely to break even, if not make a profit, a rising market having cancelled out the dealer's profit. For a further note on damage see page 494.

Introduction

From the end of the First World War, Britain reacted violently against almost any product from the nineteenth century, loosely and disparagingly termed "Victorian". The reasons for the revolt were numerous including at one extreme the emergence of new schools of thought in design and at the other, in the 1920s, the wish for, and profound belief in, a new world which would forget the war and all that preceded it and rebuild a new, albeit jazzy and slightly false, Jerusalem. New materials, new designs, new machines, new everything swept "Victorian" dust and clutter up into the attics of houses all over Britain. There most of it reposed, undisturbed, until the Second World War. Posters demanding paper, metal and cloth for the war effort were the death warrant of a great deal more attic art than actual enemy action. Rebuilding disturbed a great deal more. In the more prosperous late 1960s, there was an art market boom. Large numbers of "antique" shops opened, the majority of which had a very small percentage of antiques, in the strict sense of the hundred year rule, in their stock — but the public became aware of a vast wealth of collectable material. This was helped by several authors writing on what had previously been almost taboo subjects. Among these authors was Geoffrey Godden, who wrote a long string of excellent books including his invaluable "Victorian Porcelain", which has a useful section on marks.

Since 1971, London has had a specialist auction house for nineteenth and twentieth century works of art which has acted as a catalyst on the market. As a result of apparently high prices being obtained quite rapidly, a great number of people brought their objects to be sold, and new collectors appeared who were interested in the period. This, in turn, generated higher prices. The market is now beginning to be firmly established, although unpredictable fluctuations in price must be expected for some time.

The Victorians were wealthy, powerful and knowledgeable. They had the rare combination of technical proficiency, cheap and skilled labour and a rich consumer class who were prepared to buy modern decorative works of art, furniture and paintings. The mass production of the period meant that the lower classes could afford well designed and well made objects for the first time. Unfortunately, and this is especially true in the ceramic field, vast quantities of appallingly bad utilitarian china wares were made to fulfil demand. As they were made in great numbers, many survive and have given "Victorian" works of art a bad name.

This book starts with its roots firmly in the eighteenth century with early nineteenth century figures and wares from Derby, Rockingham and Minton harking back to the earlier century, and includes the major style changes, passing through the Gothic revival (p.178), neo-classicism (p.331), Empire (p.341), rococo (p.303), Japonaise (p.169), Art Nouveau (p.470) and Art Deco (p.110) and on to modern design with the limited editions market.

We have arranged the book according to the class of object under discussion rather than dealing with the factories separately. This will facilitate the identification of the piece, especially if one is not sure of its origin. It is also felt that a grouping of comparable objects leads to a better understanding of the factors which govern prices — the whole point of a price guide. Collectors of a particular factory should refer to the index. Here, within any particular group, the factories are arranged alphabetically and within that group again the individual pieces are listed in chronological order.

Bowls

In the eighteenth century, tea was drunk from bowls without handles, and at the end of the century, from cups. The only bowls from tea services represented on the following pages are slop bowls, used for emptying the dregs from one cup prior to a refill. This bowl is often confused with the sugar bowl or basin which should be of smaller size. When supplied with a cover, it becomes a sucrier. A single bowl from a service would have little value unless of superb quality. For prices and patterns, see the tea services section.

Large bowls are frequently one half of washing ewer and bowl sets made for masonic or other institutions but, in the first instance, they are infrequent in porcelain and, in the second, very uncommon in the nineteenth century. Bowls were also used for pot pourri and rose petals and for fruit, although at table the tazza or fruit dish took over, see table wares and plates.

It is a useful, but by no means infallible, test to support a bowl by its foot on one hand and 'ping' it with a knuckle of the other to discover whether it is cracked. It should ring true if perfect, produce a dull 'donk' if restored or a double ring if cracked. However, this is not an absolutely reliable test. A bowl which has had a semi-circular piece knocked from the rim can still ring and, if well restored, can still lead one to believe it is undamaged. Conversely, some of the moulded bowls from services of the first half of the century are of a very soft paste and sound dead even if perfect. As always, examine everything carefully before buying.

Bowls are among the most difficult of objects for a collector to display. Since the exterior usually bears most of the decoration, they have to be placed at, or above, eye level to be seen effectively.

Bowls

Belleek 1869
Diameter 10ins:25.6cm. Impressed name, moulded registration

A rare and early piece of Belleek, the lily buds and leaves tinted in pale colours.

£80–£120

Copeland c.1870
Diameter 17¾ins:45cm. Printed name

A good centrepiece in turquoise and gilding, stylistically interesting and well moulded. It has the disadvantage of being Copeland, a neglected factory, except for the parian figures, and of being rather large, more suitable for use than pure decoration.

£40–£60

Bowls

Rockingham 1830-42
Width 9ins:23cm. Printed griffin in puce

A superb painting of Wentworth House, seat of the Earl Fitzwilliam, the patron of the Rockingham factory, within a burnished gilt band and white floral encrustation. The association of the subject makes this a great deal more expensive than would be an unidentified church. Several sizes are known and with less interesting flower painting can range from £120–£200.

£500–£800

Wedgwood c.1920
Diameter 7¼ins:18.4cm. Printed vase and name

A common little bowl of a not very high standard of printing. These dragon and butterfly subjects are often erroneously referred to as 'Fairyland', which they are not.

£35–£50

Bowls

Wedgwood 1920s
Diameter 11ins:28cm. Printed vase and name

A fruit dish with flared sides decorated on the interior with complex
fairyland scenes.

£500–£600

Wedgwood 1920s
Diameter 3¾ins:9.5cm.

A rare bowl and cover with a fairyland subject. The printing of the gilding is not as sharp as it could be but the rarity of the piece will outweigh any slight production faults.

£600–£650

Bowls

Wedgwood 1920s
Diameter 10½ins:27cm. Printed vase and name

A typical fairyland bowl with panels of brightly-coloured and gilt dream folk and landscapes, the borders with gilt pebbles on a black ground. It is vital to check very carefully for restoration on fairyland lustre as the complexity of the design means that re-painting is easy to hide. A bowl has come to notice that had a triangular piece of the rim about the size of a 10p piece that had been restored but which still rang true when struck.

£300–£350

Wedgwood 1920s
Diameter 6¼ins:15.9cm. Printed vase and name

Despite the lack of fairies this is a desirable bowl as fish are rare on these lustres. The background is mottled blue with the fish coloured and gilt.

£120–£150

Bowls

Wedgwood 1920s
Diameter 10¾ins:27.6cm. Printed vase and name

Although not a particularly exciting or brilliantly coloured bowl, this is unusual in that it has the designer's, J. Makeig-Jones's, monogram incorporated in the design, raising the price from about £250–£350.

£400–£500

Wedgwood 1920s
Diameter 6¾ins:16.5cm. Printed vase and name

Uncommon, as this bowl has a red-gold ground exterior with the fairies etc., in yellow-gold and tangerine enamel. The interior in blue on a pearl lustre ground. Although uncommon and generally expensive, this type is given to great fluctuations in price.

£280–£320

Bowls

Wedgwood 1920
Diameter 9¼ins:23.5cm. Printed vase and name

A rare Persian-influenced pattern of birds and animals in trees against a sea-green lustre ground, the interior against a pearl ground. Known as the Rhages pattern.

£500–£600

Wedgwood c.1930

Diameter 7¼ins:18.4cm. Printed vase and name

A gold lustre exterior with gilt and coral fairyland scenes, the whole rather ill-defined and weak but the interior with a pearl lustre ground and a good 'art deco' roundel and border.

£400–£500

Bowls

Royal Worcester 1905
Diameter 9½ins:24.2cm. Printed crowned circle and date code

Typical of a lot of reasonable quality but boring mass-produced wares which could have been made by many factories around the turn of the century. This is a salad bowl which would originally have had electro-plated porcelain-handled servers with it. With them £20–£30.

£15–£20

Royal Worcester 1905
Diameter 9ins:22.8cm. Printed crowned circle and date code

A rather dreadful bowl with bad gilding and somewhat dirty-coloured autumn leaves and berries. Produced by any factory without the magic Worcester name, a similar bowl would be lucky to fetch only £10–£15.

£40–£50

Cabinet Objects

This section includes all the small pieces, usually of exceptional quality, which were never intended for use. It also includes items such as cups and saucers from services or small vases and figures which have since become typical cabinet objects. The Derby miniatures are examples (p. 22). There are devoted collectors of the small and the fine who are prepared to pay over the odds for good examples, and prices in this section may appear on the high side. It is arguable that many other pieces in the rest of the book could fall into this category and time will no doubt increase the numbers.

Belleek c.1870
Length 13ins:33cm. Impressed name

A masterpiece of clay latticework producing a basket and cover and further encrusted with flowers and crabstock handles, all under a shiny glaze. Very fragile and useless, the handles are uncomfortably rough and the flowers sharply moulded enough to lacerate oneself, but a decorative and interesting item.

£80–£120

Cabinet Objects

Chamberlain & Co. c.1820
Painted name

A good cup and saucer with a salmon ground enclosing scenes of
Ullswater Lake and Tonbridge Castle, probably by Thomas Baxter.
Rubbed gilding would reduce the price to £40—£80.

£80—£150

Copeland and Garrett c.1840
Gilt printed

A well decorated cup with Continental scenes within gilt scrolls on a turquoise ground. Originally part of a coffee service. The gilding tooled and of good quality, the scenes typical of the period and reflecting still the Grand Tour interest.

£20–£25

Cabinet Objects

Royal Crown Derby c.1910-c.1920
Heights 1¼ to 3¾ins:3.2 to 9.5cm.
Printed crowned monogram and date codes

Great changes have been wrought in people's collecting habits by their housing habits. Since the end of the first world war increasing numbers of people have taken to living in small flats and houses, restricting the space devotable to a collection. This has led to a miniaturization of taste and objects such as pot-lids, snuff bottles, hat pins, Goss porcelain have become very popular. The Derby Imari miniatures are now very collectable and becoming more expensive. Examples: scuttle, £20; saucepan, £30; caddy, £20; casserole, £20; jug, £15; coffee-pot, £30; teapot, £20; tyg, £10; milk churn, £30; iron and stand, £20; watering-can, £35.

Average price per piece £10–£20

Royal Crown Derby 1912
Height 6¼ins:15.8cm. Printed crowned monogram and date code

This table bell is not a common item and has the 1128 Imari pattern,the flowers in iron-red, blue, green and gilding. Miniature about the same price.

£50–£60

Cabinet Objects

G. Grainger & Co. c.1840
Height 9½in:24cm. Printed name

An uncommon biscuit porcelain bower, being decked with glazed and
coloured flowers by cupids. Because of the delicate nature of the
encrustation obviously difficult to find in good state. With a few leaves
damaged £150–£200, more damaged £80.

£200–£300

Rockingham 1830-42
Width $3\frac{3}{8}$in:8.5cm. Griffin in puce and Cl 2

A rare patch-box, the lid moulded in the shape of a butterfly and in natural colours. The box in azure blue, edged in gilt.

£200–£250

Cabinet Objects

Rockingham 1830-42
Height 8¼ins:21cm. Printed griffin in puce

An example of a bottle with well executed relief flowers, and made in other sizes and shapes.

£120–£200

Rockingham 1830-42
Height 3¾ins:9.5 cm. Printed griffin in puce

A miniature teapot with a rustic green handle and applied with coloured sprays of flowers. An uncommon object which with the magic Rockingham name and mark results in a high price, despite the almost inevitable nibbling of the flowers. A pristine example £200–£300.

£120–£150

Cabinet Objects

Swansea early 19th century
Painted name and title

A very rare cabinet cup painted by Thomas Baxter with a named view of Beaufort Cottage which was next to a Quaker meeting house. Despite damage and restoration to the scroll handle and the.naïve (bad) painting of the scene, this is a very desirable cup because of its factory and association value.

£400–£450

Royal Worcester possibly 1876
Height 9½ins:24cm. Printed with illegible code

Good quality decoration in bright enamels and gilding; obvious, but adulterated Japanese influence. Typically underpriced. The type of teapot that would have stood on the tray on p. 169.

£30–£40

Cabinet Objects

Royal Worcester 1878
Diameter of saucer 3¾ins:9.5cm. Printed crowned circle and date code

A Japanese taste cup and saucer probably not made as a cabinet item but now rarely found in services.   The handle as a chocolate and gilt dragon.

£15–£20

Royal Worcester c.1880
Impressed crowned circle

A double-walled cup and saucer, honeycomb pierced, enamelled and gilt and applied with turquoise beads. First exhibited at the 1851 exhibition by Chamberlain. A tea service of this pattern was given to Jenny Lind after her concert for the benefit of the Worcester workers. She refused it on the grounds that she could receive no payment for a charity performance. Probably the type of object that George Owen started on when he began at the factory. Jug of the same pattern £120–£150.

£150–£250

Royal Worcester 1881/2
Height 6¼ins:16cm.
Elaborate printed mark including crowned circle and registration

An exceptionally rare teapot poking fun at the Aesthetic movement and based on costumes from the Gilbert and Sullivan opera Patience. The cover in the form of two heads, one female, one male. The pot is unusually thinly cast and is of a high technical standard, the delicacy of the whole probably contributive to its scarcity. A badly damaged example sold in 1973 for £230.

£400–£600

Royal Worcester late 19th century
Height 5ins:12.7cm. Impressed crowned circle

A double-walled pierced teapot by George Owen but not signed, and with turquoise and white beading on coloured grounds and additional gilt details. Although of good quality, the lack of Owen's signature makes all the difference to the price. With it £280–£320.

£200–£220

Cabinet Objects

Royal Worcester 1890
Height 6⅜ ins:16.2cm. Printed crowned circle

A well-pierced vase by George Owen but lacking his signature. Had it been incised on the base, £250–£300.

£200–£250

Royal Worcester 1903
Height 4¼ins:10.8cm. Printed crowned circle, date code

A poor photograph of a good box by George Owen. Although not signed, the piece bears all the evidence of his hand, with crisp honeycomb piercing and good gilding. The feet are four masks and shields. An incised signature could put the price up to £350–£450.

£250–£300

Cabinet Objects

Royal Worcester 1907
Length 6½ins:16.5cm. Printed crowned circle, date code

A rare pierced slipper by George Owen and signed on the base, the cutting is exceptionally sharp and the gilding, composed of minute dots, very fine. An ideal cabinet object.

£500–£600

Royal Worcester 1919
Height 6½ins:16cm. Printed gilt mark and date code

A very elaborate box and cover by George Owen and with his incised signature on the base. Despite the fact that the knop on this particular example had been broken off and stuck back, it fetched £650 in a sale in 1973. A perfect example would fetch nearer the upper limit given.

£650–£800

Royal Worcester 1924
Printed crowned circle and date code

A good pierced cup and saucer by George Owen, the double-walled cup with his incised signature. The gilding, as always on Owen pieces, of good quality. A box and cover with piercing similar to Owen's work has been seen with a printed gilt signature but the authenticity of the piece is open to some doubt.

£400–£500

Royal Worcester Modern and 1939
Jug 1½ins:3.8cm. Printed crowned circles and date codes

Royal Worcester miniatures are popular and less common than Royal Crown Derby, although, generally speaking, of a lower standard of production. The jug is by William Powell. An older thimble with a signed scene by a good artist, £15–£60.

Thimble £4–£8, Jug £18–£25

Cache-Pots, Jardinières etc.

A favourite and exotic dessert in the summers of the first half of the nineteenth century was ice cream. Ice was cut in winter from lakes and ponds and stored in underground cellars in the gardens of the larger country houses where it would last until the following autumn. The actual production of the dessert is outside the scope of this book, but was a wrist-breaking exercise and well worth reading in contemporary recipe books. To be brought to the table, the ice cream was transferred to a double-walled pail with cover, the container with the cream resting in a bucket of crushed ice and salt. In the days before refrigeration, this must have been a real treat. These pails are now frequently used to contain ice for drinks or, without cover and liner, they are used as jardinières.

The jardinière is a bowl, usually with a flat base, in which to grow plants indoors, whereas a cache-pot is of a more fixed form being a tapering cylinder in which to hide the common or garden earthenware flowerpot. This enables one to have a succession of flowering plants all the year round in the same decorative container. Both are found with stands.

A bowl, usually oval, with a wavy rim was either a glass cooler or has taken its form from one. The set of glasses was inverted in the bowl of iced water, the stems resting in the notches, to chill before drinking hock or other white wines. These are now more usually found described as jardinières.

Belleek 1870—1880
Diameter 10ins:25.5cm. Printed symbol and name

A good cache-pot with crisply modelled flowers at the mouth, the sides with moulded prunus blossom. Several petals are missing from this example as is almost inevitable but a perfect piece £100—£150.

£70—£100

Cache-Pots, Jardinières

Probably Coalport Mid-19th century
Diameter 4ins:10cm. Simulated Sèvres mark

Probably made as wine glass coolers but usually known now as jardinières or cache pots. This pair of very fine quality with tooled gilding and rich fruit and figure painting. Many English factories in the first half of the 19th century used a simulated Sèvres mark and it has been stated, possibly wrongly, that English artists decorated on 18th century Sèvres bodies, which would explain the close similarity sometimes found in the paste. A genuine factory mark of Minton or Coalport could add 20%–30% to the value.

£250–£300

Minton c.1850
Diameter 9ins:22.8cm. No mark

A jardinière with rather stiff exotic birds within gilt borders on the bleu-de-roi ground. Loosely based on an 18th century Sèvres original. The attribution to Minton is founded on the style of bird painting which is known on marked examples from this factory. A pair, £200–£300.

£70–£100

Moore 1868—1875
Diameter 10ins:25.4cm. Impressed name and retailer's mark

A well cast jardinière with lilies against a turquoise ground, the neck with black and gilt key-fret. Much better quality than most of Moore's production which tends to be left uncoloured, exposing a finely crackled creamy glaze. This example bears the retailer's mark of Thomas Goode which may account for the higher standard.

£40—£60

Rockingham c.1830-42
Height 6½ins:16.5cm. Printed griffin in puce

A very rare pair of cache-pots attractively painted with panels of flowers. The rest of the body deep blue and gilt. Quite apart from the attractive painting of these cache-pots making them desirable, the factory made very few of them.

£300–£400

Cache-Pots, Jardinières

Swansea c.1820
Height 5ins:12.7cm. No mark

Although unmarked, the form, without the feet, is known. The decoration is loosely based on a Chinese original and is in a famille-rose palette.

£40—£50

Royal Worcester 1899
Diameter 13¼ins:33.5cm.
Printed crowned circle, registration and date code

A large cache-pot with well cast high relief green and brown lion masks and scrolls against the usual yellow/apricot ground. Size is of major importance in the price of jardinières, a similar 10ins:25.5cm. example would fetch £80–£100.

£120–£180

Cache-Pots, Jardinières

Royal Worcester 1901
Diameter 14ins:35.5cm. Printed crowned circle, date code

Another large cache-pot, printed and coloured with flowers on a
yellowish ground, the shoulders with lightly moulded panels of masks
and scrolls slightly gilt. A similar example entirely hand-painted with
flowers would be £150–£200 and with scenes by H. Stinton,
£250–£400.

£120–£150

Royal Worcester 1903

Diameter 13¾ins:35cm.
Printed, crowned circle registration and date code

A fine pair of cache-pots with apple-green rims and bases. The too small panels by Harry Davis, signed. Had the panels been larger they would fetch considerably more.

£500–£700

Cache-Pots, Jardinières

Unattributed c.1850
Width 14½ins:36cm. Pseudo Sèvres interlaced Ls

One of a good pair of ormolu-mounted jardinières, the bowl after a
Sèvres original with well painted flowers reserved on a gilt-pebbled,
sky-blue ground. There has been much inconclusive discussion on the
factory(s) that produced this imitation Sèvres. At one time it was
thought to be original 18th century Sèvres porcelain decorated in this
country, though this now seems unlikely; certainly a great deal of old
Sèvres was redecorated in France. Otherwise it can be attributed to
Madeley, Minton, Coalport or several other possibilities, all of which
made similar pastes.

£200–£300.

Figures, Busts

Figures were among the first objects produced in Europe after the invention of porcelain and have been popular ever since. Their appeal is obvious, which is the criticism levelled at them by those who collect wares. The nineteenth century saw figures produced in the severely classical, the wildly rococo and the highly stylised moulds – a collection of a long surviving factory throughout the period would be a strange hotchpotch indeed.

The subjects from the first half of the century are often debased eighteenth century models of shepherds and shepherdesses, mythological, literary or royal figures, political or ecclesiastical contemporaries, many of them in biscuit porcelain or parian. Animal models, especially dogs, were popular and continue so. Although most of these were produced in pottery, some fine porcelain examples are found.

A large number of the so-called Staffordshire pottery figures of the 1820-50 period are in fact porcelain and one has been included as an example on p.124. The subject will be fully covered in a forthcoming Price Guide to 19th Century Pottery. The method of production is described on p.155.

The entry of the limited edition figure market, which has boomed since its introduction in the 1940s has brought a new element into the already difficult job of trying to estimate the price an object might fetch at auction. It is now quite possible for an edition to be over subscribed, completed, and for an example immediately offered for sale to rise in price from £1,500 to £11,700 – as in fact happened with the Ronald Van Ruyckvelt doves. The movement seems to be towards a stock market situation with people virtually selling the certificate and taking possession of a box without ever unpacking, let alone displaying, the contents. I suspect the day cannot be far off when we move into a commodity situation with 'collectors' speculating in futures, selling off for a profit their rights to an order placed for a model before having received it or even paid for it.

At this point, those whose expertise lies in the field of ceramics begin to lose control of the situation and the financial wizards take over. One hopes that they are more successful than those in 1970 who scalded their fingers badly when the 'silver coffee-pot bubble' burst.

Samuel Alcock and Co. 1828
Height 8½ins:21.4cm. Printed beehive and name

A fine and rare pair of busts of George IV and the Duke of York uncoloured and unglazed, but the plinths glazed and with matt gilt lines. Busts of this quality at this date are not frequently met with and are mainly collected by the devotees of portrait and commemorative wares. These would appeal also to those interested in ceramic history as they were recalled shortly after issue for 'the infringement of certain rights'.

£300–£350

Samuel Alcock and Co. 1840—50
Height 7½ins:19cm. Printed and impressed name

A small and attractive pair of parian figure groups of fine quality, the intricacy of the modelling indicating that a large number of moulds would have been employed, perhaps thirty to fifty for each figure. Obviously uncommon to find undamaged in any way. Their style harks back to 18th century figures, making them less desirable to the parian purist who would concentrate on obvious 19th century models.

£80—£120

John Bevington 1872-92
Length 8¾ins:22.2cm. Painted JB in underglaze blue

One of the smaller factories that in the second half of the 19th century specialised in good copies of other, earlier products, these being after Meissen originals. The figures well-modelled and coloured, and with gilt details.

£120–£200

Brownfield and Co. last quarter of the 19th century
Height 9¾ins:25cm. Impressed name

One of a pair of figures entitled Mama and Papa as children dressed in their parents' clothes, the boy in top hat, boots and with an umbrella. Figures of sickening sentimentality relieved only by the interest of the contemporary clothing and as a comment on the attitude to the children of the time.

£10–£15

Figures, Busts,

Brownfield and Co. 1899
Height 11ins:28cm. Printed globes and date code

A late flowering of the Japanese taste in the form of two vases attended by geishas, all in pale enamels and gilding. The standard of production is high and the subject is mildly amusing but Brownfield is not a highly rated or collected factory, although they were much praised in the Art Journals of the time.

£100–£120

Chamberlain c.1827
Height 5ins:12.8cm. Painted name

A very rare and fine set of the Tyrolese group of singers, the Rainers, who toured England in 1827 and 1828. They were originally sold for £2 the set. Single figures £120–£150.

£1,200–£1,800

Figures, Busts

Copeland 1846
Height 12ins:30.5cm. Impressed name, printed title

An early parian figure of Narcissus after John Gibson, R.A. and so entitled. It was modelled by E.B. Stephens for the Art Union of London as their first parian figure. Fifty copies were produced, all to be given as prizes in their lottery. Uncommon. Later examples £80–£150.

£150–£200

Copeland 1860s
Height 13ins:33cm. Impressed Copeland

A scarce group of Florence Nightingale tending a wounded soldier, a ribbon on her breast entitled Scutari. This example has broken hand and stick accounting for the low price. In good condition £150–£180. The original marble by T. Phyffers was exhibited at the Royal Academy in 1857.

£50–£80 (damaged)

Figures, Busts

Copeland 1862
Height 17¼ins:44cm. Impressed name and date

Victorian sculpture and parian figures are frequently distressingly sentimental to our eyes but can sometimes be quite charming like this group entitled on the base: Go to Sleep. After a model by J. Durham for the Art Union of London, both pieces of information cast into the base.

£50–£70

Copeland c.1865
Height 16¾ins:42.5cm. Impressed and printed names

The famous Tinted Venus after John Gibson R.A. holding her golden apple. The original marble aroused a storm of protest as the sculptor lightly coloured her for the 1862 International Exhibition. It was issued by the Art Union of Great Britain.

£60–£90

Figures, Busts

Copeland 1874
Height 21¾ins:51.2cm. Impressed name and date code

After the marble by Raphael Monti, with a moulded signature and the
title, Nora Creena. Monti was a much lauded sculptor who showed at
the major International Exhibitions, his special skill being the
suggestion of features beneath gauze or drapery. Many of his busts and
figures were transmuted into parian.

£70–£100

Copeland and Garrett 1833-47
Height 7¾ins:19.7cm. Printed and impressed name

An uncommon pair of 'Felspar porcelain' busts of Locke and Ben Johnson. Felspar porcelain was one of many new bodies produced between the beginning and middle of the 19th century. These busts are no great advertisement for the material, since they both display unfortunate blotchy discoloration. An unspotty pair £50–£80.

£30–£50

Copeland and Garrett 1833-47
Length 11½ins:29cm. Printed name

An uncommonly good pair of greyhounds coloured in grey and cream and brown, the base lime-green and gilt. In a completely different class from the more usual Staffordshire pottery examples and, due to their large size, highly decorative as well. 6ins:15.2cm. pair £100–£150.

£400–£450

Royal Crown Derby 1969
Height 5¼ins:13.3cm.
Printed factory marks and limitation number

One of 250 red and gilt dragons made to commemorate the Investiture of the Prince of Wales at Caernarvon Castle. It was originally issued at £52. 10s. 0d.

£120–£180

Royal Doulton c.1910
Height 7ins:17.8cm. Printed mark in black

A titled portrait figure of the actor W.C. Penley as Charley's Aunt. Penley produced Charley's Aunt in 1892 when it ran for 1,466 performances. Because of its theatrical interest, it is more likely to be popular with a Staffordshire figure collector concentrating on the theatre.

£25—£35

Royal Doulton c.1920
Height 8ins:20.3cm. Printed mark and painted title

A typical Naughty Twenties figure of the Bather disrobing, the robe in brilliant purple with blue lining, uncovering her pink skin, her hair golden.

£30–£40

Royal Doulton 1920s
Height 8ins: 20.3cm. Printed mark and painted title

An amusing figure evocative of the period. The girl in fancy dress with bright red collar, polychrome interior to the cloak and black cat suit, entitled Marietta. Along with Royal Worcester figures of this period, not yet greatly in demand.

£30—£50

Goss and Peake 1867
Height 26ins:66cm. Incised names

A rare and large parian bust of Dickens. Goss was only for a short time working with Peake, a roofing tile manufacturer. William Gallimore who modelled the bust and whose name is also incised on the back, left Goss to work at Belleek in 1863 along with several other workers but returned to continue with Goss. The over-large size of the bust has affected the price; it should, because of its rarity, fetch much more.

£100–£120

Figures, Busts

W.H. Goss c.1880
Heights 16½ and 17ins:41.9 and 43.2cm. Printed name

A fine pair of figures with refined coloration and gilding. A high price as they are much sought after by Goss collectors and parian figure collectors, as well as being suitable for the decorator market.

£250–£300

H.T. & Co. mid 19th century
Height 15¼ins:38.7cm. Incised H.T. & Co

A well cast group of Eliezer and Rebecca. A large number of Old Testament subjects were made in parian. The factory does not seem to be recorded.

£80–£120

Figures, Busts

J. Hadley and Sons 1903
Height 9ins: 23cm. Printed crowned circle, date code

A well modelled and coloured group in shot silk and gold by James
Hadley. The character on the left is not Alexander Solzhenitsyn but
Paul Kreuger of South Africa, the other is Neville Chamberlain. Other
groups include other contemporary politicians.

£150–£200

DON QUIXOTTE

SANCHA PANZA

Minton c.1830
Heights 5½ and 4¾ins:14 and 12cm. No mark

A very rare pair of figures which appear to pre-date the Staffordshire 'flat-backs' in that they are hollow at the rear. Don Quixote has a loop to accommodate a wooden or metal lance. The modelling and colouring are of a high standard and like all Minton figures of this date they are by no means frequently met with. The spelling of the names varies.

£250–£350

Minton 1835
Height 7½ins:19cm. No mark

Well coloured and gilt figures with a great deal of charm, considerably rarer than for example 18th century Chelsea gardeners, but despite this much less expensive. Watch out for restoration to early Minton figures; they seem particularly vulnerable to damage.

£150–£250

Minton c.1835
Height 9ins:23cm. No mark

A pair of the same figures opposite, shown mounted as candlesticks with encrusted flowers and elaborate bases. Most early nineteenth century figures can be found with variations in casting, positioning and painting, and, assuming the quality and condition are consistent, there is little change in the price. Any great elaboration, as h ere, makes a difference.

£220–£280

Minton c.1848
Height 6¾ins:17cm. No mark

An early parian figure following the tradition of the biscuit porcelain models. It was issued with a companion £80–£120, and coloured £100–£150.

£30–£50

Minton c.1840
Heights 3¾ and 4ins:9.6 and 10.1cm. No mark

A rare pair of figures forming candle snuffers, their clothes brightly painted and gilt. These were also made to fit on the base of an elaborate 'bower' candlestick. With the candlesticks £500–£600. Very infrequently found in good condition due to the softness of the body.

£200–£300

Minton c.1840
Height 8¾ins:21cm. No mark

A well-decorated figure of a guitar player seated, rather oddly, on a copy of a Chinese garden seat. All well enamelled and gilt. Pair with dancer £250–£300.

£80–£150

Minton c.1840
Height 8¾ins:21cm. No mark

A richly decorated and well modelled pair of sweetmeat figures on gilt rococo bases. The Minton painting on figures of this date was second to none in elaboration and they are last gasp of the 18th century figure tradition.

£300—£400

Minton c.1845
Height 13¼ins:33.6cm. Incised ermine mark

An early group of good quality representing Naomi and her daughters-in-law, which was shown as the 1851 Exhibition. Large models of this type in good condition are beginning to be sought after. Damage affects the price dramatically.

£90—£120

Minton 1858
Height 13¾ins:35cm. Impressed Minton and date cypher

Sir Colin Campbell, Baron Clyde, 1792-1873; served in China, India and the West Indies. He also commanded a division in the Crimea and suppressed the Indian Mutiny. This figure is by MacBride and also dated 1858.

£40–£60

Figures, Busts

Minton 1858
Height 14½ins:36.8cm. Impressed marks and date cypher

Another MacBride figure; this of Sir Henry Havelock, 1795-1857, who figures largely in the Indian Mutiny with Sir Colin Campbell. With the rise in interest in Staffordshire portrait figures and the belated appreciation of parian as a material, these portrait figures are rising in price.

£30—£60

Minton 1863
Height 21½ins: 54.5cm. Impressed name with date code

A large group entitled 'Daniel Saved', after the original by W. Beattie.

£60–£80

Minton 1955
Height 6ins:15.3cm. Printed crowned globe and titles

Three from a set of the ten Queen's Beasts after originals by James Woodford O.B.E., R.A. Each brightly coloured and gilt and issued in sets in 1955 in an edition of 150. They also formed part of the Coronation (1953) vase which was formed by contribution from the major Staffordshire factories. The quality is good and the set has appreciated considerably in the last ten years.

£650–£700 (set of 10)

Robinson and Leadbeater c.1885
Heights 14 and 14½ins:37 and 36.5cm. Impressed initials

A decorative pair of coloured figures of Italian children of a high standard of both modelling and colouring, some of the details gilt. The use of enamelling on parian makes these figures closely resemble hard paste coloured biscuit figures from the Paris factories; so care should be taken in establishing their pedigree.

£100–£150

Figures, Busts

Rockingham 1826-30
Height 7⅞ ins:19.4cm. Griffin in red and incised No. 42

Rockingham figures were produced both in biscuit and coloured in the pre and post 1830 period. This figure of Napoleon in a green coat with gilt braided epaulettes and medals and red cuffs and collar is very rare, as indeed are most Rockingham figures.

£400–£500

Rockingham 1826-42
Height $3\frac{7}{8}$ ins: 9.8cm.
Impressed Rockingham Works Brameld. Incised No. 136 and C1 2 in red

Many Rockingham and Derby animal figures are virtually identical, probably because the Rockingham factory hired Derby modellers. The incised numbers however vary and, in the absence of any other mark, serve to differentiate the factories. Rockingham pugs and cats are the most frequently found, though not common, but peacocks are exceptionally rare. Uncoloured but for green patches on the base and gilt details.

£250–£300 as shown. £300–£500 perfect

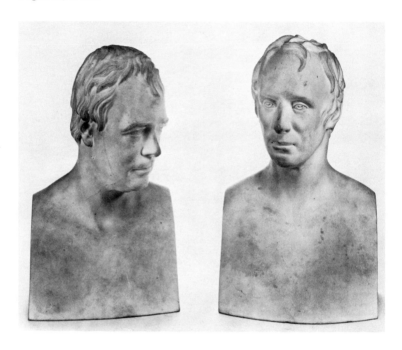

Rockingham 1826-42
Height 7½ins: 19cm. Impressed griffin

A rare pair of biscuit porcelain busts of Scott and Wordsworth. Not the most attractive of objects but nevertheless very saleable because of their rarity.

£350–£400

Royal Worcester 1865
Heights 7½ to 7¾ins: 19 and 19.8cm. Printed crowned circle

A pair of spill vase putti influenced by Capo di Monte originals. Each strongly coloured and gilt and of quite surprising unattractiveness. It is worth noting that any figures which are posed to look downwards are difficult to display satisfactorily and result in a low price.

£60–£100

Royal Worcester c.1865
Height 13ins:33cm. Printed crowned circle

A parian group of Henda and Hafed, not common in good condition.

£60–£80

Royal Worcester c.1870
Height 12ins:30.5cm. Printed crowned circle

Originally produced during the Kerr and Binns period, 1852-1862. These and the other busts produced during this time were generally of fine quality. They are also known with turquoise beading and gilt details, £100–£120.

£80–£120

Figures, Busts

Royal Worcester c.1870
Heights 10½ and 11ins: 26.7 and 27.9cm. Impressed crowned circle

Both in powder-blue and gilt dresses and with uncoloured bodies, called
"before the wind" and "against the wind". They can, like many of
these models be found coloured (£200–£250), in celadon
(£100–£120), or white (£80–£120).

£150–£200

Royal Worcester 1874
Height 6¾ins:16cm. Impressed crowned circle and registration

One of a set of six menu-holders of down-and-outs which are now much sought after. Although presumably issued in sets, some are much rarer than others. They include a peg-legged war veteran, a Frenchman in beret and boys with hands in pockets. Their colouring varies considerably from white £40—£50, though quite well coloured like this example, to a few of a very high standard £120—£180.

£100—£150

Royal Worcester c.1875
Height 18ins:45.6cm. Impressed crowned circle

Despite the quality of this piece, it is too large and out of the ordinary for the average Worcester collector, therefore selling to the interior decorator market. About £40–£60 uncoloured.

£150–£200

Royal Worcester last quarter of the 19th century
Height 17¾ins:45cm. Impressed crowned circle

A rare pug dog of exceptionally large size, naturalistically coloured in matt enamels. There are, for no apparent reason, devoted pug dog collectors who are prepared to pay over the odds for unusual examples and with the demand from Worcester addicts this has become an expensive model. Being matt glazed and of a 'muddy' coloration, restoration is particularly difficult to spot.

£300–£350

Figures, Busts

Royal Worcester 1886
Height 6½ins:16.5cm. Printed crowned circle, date code

A figure of a Russian, tinted ivory only, a more desirable coloured example £80—£120. One of a series of eleven countries of the world. The full set, all in similar colours, would be of exceptional interest.

£40—£60

Royal Worcester 1888
Height 8½ins:21.6cm. Printed crowned circle including date code

One of a pair of so-called Kate Greenaway candlestick figures, after James Hadley. Hadley probably produced about thirty of these figures and several as candlesticks. Their prim innocence appeals to many collectors. Pair £150–£250. Uncoloured pair £60–£100.

£30–£60

Figures, Busts

Royal Worcester 1889
Height 6¾ins:17.3cm.
Printed crowned circle, registration and date code

A sweetmeat basket figure, possibly after Hadley, palely coloured. At first glance, this figure could equally be by Minton, Brownfield or Moore, when it would, however, be less expensive. A pair £120–£150.

£50–£70

Royal Worcester 1891
Heights 11¼ins. and 12½ins:28.5cm. and 31.8cm.
Printed crowned circle and impressed marks

A good pair of Turkish water carrier figures decorated in shot enamels and complete with the bowls and detachable liners. These are usually missing, which affects the price by £10–£20. As with most Worcester figures the quality varies considerably.

£300–£400

Figures, Busts

Royal Worcester 1892
Height 8½ins:21.5cm.
Printed crowned circle, date code and registration

Described in the factory shape book as Bringaree Indians although they
look suspiciously like Turks. A good pair and not common, shot enamel
coloration. In white £50–£80.

£180–£220

Royal Worcester 1898
Height 21¾ins:55.5cm.
Printed crowned circle, registration and date code

A large and well decorated figure, her robe in gilt-sheened green on blue-tinged base. The large size and the fact that she is supporting something on her head make her ideally suited for conversion into a table lamp. There is, however, no central hole for the flex and an example drilled for electricity would be reduced in value to £100–£120. Damage on a suitable case for conversion to another purpose affects the value less than on a simple cabinet item.

£150–£200

Figures, Busts

Royal Worcester 1898
Height 19½ins:49.5cm. Printed crowned circle with date code

A rare figure of very large size, coloured in shot enamels and gilding. A figure such as this would probably go to the interior decorator as much as to the Worcester collector. Damage to the violin, for example, with a restored hand could reduce the price to £250–£400.

£500–£600

Royal Worcester 1899
Heights 12 and 12¼ins:30.5 and 31.1cm.
Printed crowned circle, registration and date code

Palely coloured with gilt flower scrolls. With models having fine detail such as the fingers free-standing it is worth checking carefully, before buying, for damage and restoration.

£170–£220

Figures, Busts

Royal Worcester 1904
Heights 5½ and 6½ins: 14 and 16.5cm.
Printed crowned circle with date code

A pair of water carrier figures decorated in shot enamels, late examples of the shape 637 first issued in 1876 but nevertheless sharply cast.

£150–£200

Royal Worcester 1911
Height 25¼ins:64.2cm. Printed crowned circle, date code

An exceptionally large figure of the Bather Surprised, lightly coloured and gilt. In this case the size is overpowering with a proportionally low price. A 15ins. example would fetch about the same.

£150–£200

Figures, Busts

Royal Worcester 1919
Height 9¾ins:24.8cm. Printed crowned circle with date code

An example of poor moulding and uninteresting gilding, otherwise an attractive figure. A sharp, tinted example £70–£120. Too little consideration is paid at the present to the difference between good and bad examples of the same figure. This is a late casting of a figure originally issued in the 1860s and is one of a pair of Joy and Sorrow, this one being Joy. Pair of these £120–£150, good pair £150–£200.

£50–£70

Royal Worcester 1930s
Height 8½ins:21.5cm. Printed crowned circle

One of a series of fourteen children representing the days of the week, this Tuesday's Boy, by Freda Doughty. Other models by Dorothy's sister include the months of the year and nursery rhymes. They are still made today £12–£18.

£20–£30

Figures, Busts

Royal Worcester 1930s
Height 7ins:17.8cm. Printed crowned circle

A rare pair of art deco figures of musicians from a set of four. Very much of their period these 20s and 30s figures should be more seriously collected and higher priced, especially since the majority are uncommon.

£100–£150

Royal Worcester 1930s
Height 3ins:7.8cm. Printed crowned circle

Leopard cubs from a series of 'zoo babies' by Doris Lindner. Although most appealing, the series was not popular at the time and examples are rare.

£80–£120

Figures, Busts

Royal Worcester 1931
Height 5¼ins: 13.3cm. Printed crowned circle mark and date code

An 'art deco' model of a sleeping doe, modelled by Eric Aumonier. Enamelled in grey-blue and emerald. Uncommon and underpriced.

£30–£50

Royal Worcester 1933
Height 5½ins:14cm. Printed crowned circle, date code, painted title

The Old Goat Woman, after a model by Phoebe Stabler, brightly coloured and underpriced. The pattern number on the base of this particular model does not fit with the factory records, the correct number being 2886, not 2896 which was a calf by Stella Crofts.

£60–£80

Royal Worcester 1935
Height 9ins:22.8cm. Printed crowned circle, title, date code

Pair of figures of King George V and Queen Mary, modelled by
Gwendolin Parnell and coloured by Daisy Rea, limited edition of about
72. Not very desirable figures as, for Worcester, they are rather badly
executed, but the increasing interest in commemorative wares should
see a rise in price.

£80–£120

Royal Worcester 1937
Height 9½ins:24.5cm. Printed crowned circle, date code

An example of the rarest of all Dorothy Doughty's bird models – the Indigo Bunting. Made to be a cheap Christmas present, its lack of flowers and foliage resulted in a market failure with only six or seven being made.

£2,000–£3,000

Figures, Busts

Royal Worcester 1958
Height 10¼ins:26cm.
Printed crowned circle, facsimile signature, date

A very fine pair of Cactus Wrens on Prickly Pears, attractively modelled
and coloured and larger than most of the American series, making them
popular and expensive.

£3,000–£5,000

Royal Worcester 1960
Height 11½ins:29.3cm. Full printed marks

Lieut.-Col. H.M. Llewellyn, C.B.E., on Foxhunter, after the model by Doris Lindner. Although it might appear that the horse's left ear has been damaged, this actually was how the horse looked, his ear having been bitten by a stable companion.

£450–£600

Royal Worcester 1961
Heights 12 and 10¼ins:30.5 and 26.7cm.
Printed crowned circle, date code

A pair of Hooded Warblers on Cherokee Rose from Dorothy Doughty's American series of birds. The American series are generally more desirable than the English and the birds do not have certificates which are necessary for a good price in the majority of limited editions. Compare with the same birds uncoloured following. Single birds can be bought from about £200 in this series, coloured, and £100 plain.

£2,500–£3,000

Royal Worcester 1961
Heights 11¼ and 9½ins:28.5 and 24.1cm.
Printed crowned circle, date code

Like all the Doughty birds the mark includes a printed facsimile signature of the artist. Note the discrepancy in size with the previous pair, caused by slightly different casting and construction by the 'caster' — the correct name for the worker who assembles the birds.

£400–£500

Royal Worcester 1964
Height 17¼ins:44cm.
Printed crowned circle, title, facsimile signature, date

One of Dorothy Doughty's less popular models from the English series, the Chiff-Chaff on Hogweed. Because of the fragility of the flowers it tends to be found with a certain amount of damage. One of 500.

£400–£500

Royal Worcester 1965
Height 9¾ins:24.7cm. Full printed marks

Hyperion, after Doris Lindner, one of an edition of 500, as was Arkle, but the difference in price is worth noting.

£220–£300

Royal Worcester 1967
Height 9½ins:24cm. Full printed, including signature and date

The famous racehorse Arkle modelled by Doris Lindner. Coloured chestnut and brown with silver shoes, one of an edition of 500. The wide bracket figures reflect the unstable market for limited editions. It is rumoured that the horse has changed hands privately for well over the upper figure.

£600–£2,000 +

Royal Worcester 1968
Height 11½ins:29.9cm.
Full printed mark, including signature and date

Prince Philip on a polo pony, after Doris Lindner, one of 750. Remember that the reins of horses, when porcelain, on these models are applied after firing with araldite which is then hardened in a low temperature oven. They will, therefore, appear as restoration under an ultra-violet (black) light.

£350–£500

Royal Worcester 1968
Height 6¼ins:15.8cm.
Printed crowned circle, title and facsimile signature

A group of Charlotte and Jane after the model by Ruth Van Ruyckevelt, one of a popular series of Victorian figures issued in editions of 500. This originally cost £290. They were all issued with certificates and these must be present to ensure a good price.

£300–£500

Unattributed c.1845
Height 14¼ins:36.5cm. No mark

A good group of The Golden Age, the girl lacking a few fingers and the body slightly discoloured, nevertheless probably underpriced at the moment.

£60—£80

Figures, Busts

Unattributed c.1850—60
Height 10ins:25.4cm. No mark

At first sight a typical Staffordshire pottery figure but like so many, in
fact made of porcelain. Generally those made before the middle of the
century are better moulded, better painted and in porcelain. The very
dark underglaze-blue of the poetess's bodice is typical as is the
impressed name from printer's type. This figure is given as an example
only and the whole subject will be fully dealt with in the forthcoming
Price Guide to Staffordshire figures.

£35—£60

Figures, Busts

Unattributed, second half of the 19th century
Height 17¼ins:43.8cm. No mark

Perseus, the Greek hero, drawing his sword. A dull figure in an unsatisfactory body that has browned and stained with time. Groups that have suffered from this immovable staining are as unpopular as those with damage. However, when selling a group a great deal can be added to the price by giving it a thorough cleaning, an overnight soak in liquid bleach makes a radical difference.

£60–£80

Unattributed 1884
Height 17½ins:44.5cm. Moulded signature

A rare figure, well cast and coloured, of a tennis player with the moulded signature R.J. Morris, 1884. This example has restored hand and racket. A perfect example with lady partner £80–£150.

£18–£25 (damaged)

Jugs, Mugs and Ewers

The moulded jugs of the 1830s to 50s were cheap to buy, decorative and popular. They were often well designed by famous artists, but less frequently well cast. The material for the body was by no means fixed and one design can be found in soft earthenware, stoneware and parian; in fact, it is occasionally difficult to decide between the last two, the body looking like a fine stoneware or a proto-parian body. Those illustrated on p. 146 could be examples of these and the price would be about the same for each assuming the quality of casting was constant. An earthenware example would be considerably less, mainly due to the lack of definition. Colouring was occasionally undertaken, either self-colour in sage, pale blue or buff, or enamelled over the design, often to the detriment of the piece, but superb examples do turn up and are unlikely to fetch as much as they should. Indeed, the whole of the moulded jug market is in need of more serious consideration. One could predict that there would shortly be a sharp rise in price for good examples.

Also neglected are the porcelain jugs and mugs produced as gifts for retiring mine owners, christening presents, records of marriages or dedications of the heart with appropriate gilt script, messages, bright flowers and occasional emblems. The factories that produced them remain anonymous, as do the decorators, but a collection of the different types of person to whom and by whom they were given would show a fascinating cross section of Victorian sentiment. Most important of all, they are nearly always dated.

Large ewers from washing sets are not common in porcelain, most being made of earthenware. Those that do occur are rarely of much value since little regard was paid to them. They are, however, very good for flower decoration. Jugs from tea and coffee services are dealt with under that heading.

Samuel Alcock and Co. c.1845
Height 14½ins:37cm. Printed initials

Samuel Alcock made a large number of classically-influenced wares
from the 1840s-60s. The majority of the products were in stoneware
and will be dealt with in the forthcoming *Price Guide to 19th century
English Pottery*. The colours used here are a typical royal-blue ground
and a transfer-printed black outline, peach and orange coloured. One of
the problems that Alcock's porcelain suffers from is visible in the
photograph — the ground colour is too thin and soft with the result
that it wears badly.

£10–£15

W. Brownfield 1863
Height 7¼ins:18.4cm. Elaborate moulded mark and registration

A crisply moulded parian jug commemorating the marriage of Albert Edward, later Edward VII, to Princess Alexandra of Denmark. A well designed piece possibly by W. Harry Rogers. It is less commonly found with the background enamelled, usually in buff or chocolate, badly applied and fired, but a superb example has been noted raising the price to £15–£20. The price differential should be greater. Further moulded commemorative jugs will be found in the forthcoming *Price Guide to Commemorative Pottery*.

£10–£15

Caughley/Coalport first quarter of the 19th century
Height 8¾ins: 22.3cm. No mark

A rare pair of jugs with good flower painting and a gilt JH in a wreath, the bodies cabbage-leaf moulded, probably from 18th century moulds, and with gilt mask spouts. The Caughley factory sold out to Coalport in 1799.

£150–£180

Chinese decorated E & C Challinor 1862–80
Height 12¼ins:31cm. Overpainted printed name

A very rare 'freak'. An English Staffordshire porcelain jug decorated in Canton. It is almost impossible to explain the reason for its existence; possibly it was a sample sent from England to test the possibility of utilising the cheap labour for decorating in China, or it may have been sent by a member of a ship's company on the spot. It is probably the only example, but even so, not of much value.

£60–£200

Coalport first half of the 19th century
Height 11½ins:29.5cm. No mark

A quite well moulded and painted jug but difficult to display. Good for flowers. Originally from a bedroom washing set.

£35—£45

Copeland mid-19th century
10⅛ ins: 25.7cm. Impressed name and C.P. Art Union

An exceptionally high quality parian goblet with matt and burnished decoration. With the interest in parian being revived, at the present mainly in busts and figures, it will probably not be long before really good wares such as this rise fast in price.

£60–£70

Possibly Davenport c.1835
Height 4ins:10.1cm. No mark

A hand-painted mug with pink cabbage roses and gilt leaves. Attractive but not sought after.

£8–£12

Doulton 1897
Height 6¾ins:17.2cm. Printed green rosette

A good quality Diamond Jubilee piece with the additional interest of an inscription on the side recording its presentation to J.C. Bailey from Sir Henry Doulton. Had the mug been anything but commemorative, but with the same dedication, it would probably have fetched more.

£40–£60

J. Green 1851
Height 6¾ins:17cm. Printed name and registration

An interesting jug with a black transferred view of the 1851 Exhibition building (the Crystal Palace). Apart from pot-lids, the Exhibition wares are strangely unappreciated. Much rarer than coronation commemoratives and mostly of better quality. Should be more expensive.

£10–£15

Charles Meigh c.1846
Height 7½ins:19cm. Moulded name and registration

A 'Gothic' jug moulded in stoneware and therefore not strictly entitled to appear in this book at all but it serves to show how similar these jugs are to the parian examples. The price of a similar example in parian would be about the same but less sharp moulding could reduce the price to £2.

£10–£15

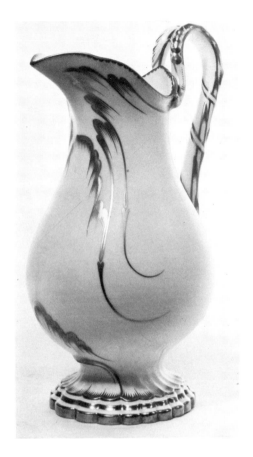

Minton 1840–50
Height 9¾ins:24.5cm. No mark

Described in the Minton shape book as a "Sèvres Ewer" since the shape is based on a Sèvres original, this jug is well moulded and gilt but of an unappreciated period and not flamboyant enough to fetch a high price.

£30–£40

Paragon 1937(6)
Height 9½ins:24cm. Elaborate gilt mark including name

A well-printed coloured design commemorating the non-event Coronation of Edward VIII. This is a limited edition of five hundred numbered on the base and in a fitted box. Most commemorative wares since 1902 were issued in vast quantities, often given to school children as souvenirs along with the one-day holiday. These were cherished by their owners and have entered the family folk history usually on the theme that only three were made, one of which is in a museum, one in America and theirs is the other. The truth is that they survive in quantity and are usually sold for between £1–£3, only the special editions fetching more.

£40–£60

Rockingham 1830-42
Height 6½ins:16.5cm. Printed griffin in puce

The handle of this mug is in the unusual form of a horse's hoof and the upper part a horse's tail, which is unique to Rockingham. Many such mugs occur unmarked but can be differentiated from almost identical Derby mugs, in that the latter do not have the upper part of the handle as a tail, i.e. moulded to simulate hair, but are quite smooth.

The mug illustrated is very rare and extremely well painted with a portrait of the Duke of Wellington in a gilt panel on a claret ground. Altogether the quality, subject matter, factory and condition add up to an expensive piece of porcelain. A crack would reduce the price to a quarter or less.

Unmarked mugs may be £10–£20 according to subject, whilst marked mugs of less documentary importance than the one illustrated are £30–£60.

£800–£1,000

Royal Worcester 1881
Height 9¼ins:23.5cm. Printed crowned circle, date code

Royal Worcester at its bizarre best. A rose-water sprinkler, vaguely Persian-influenced. The gilt ground painted with squirrels and birds and all of high quality.

£120–£150

Royal Worcester 1887
Height 9¼ins:23.5cm. Printed crowned circle, date code

The dragon handle is loosely based on the chih-lung that crawls round
the shoulders of Chinese Canton-decorated vases of the 1860s on. Not a
particularly good example with heavy-handed gilding on brown leaves.

£40–£60

Royal Worcester 1889
Height 8ins:20.2cm. Printed crowned circle, date code

A neatly and attractively painted pair of jugs with named views of the Rhine and Black Mountain NA, framed by gilt leaves. The upper handle terminal is in the form of a dolphinesque bird's head. Touches of this sort add to the desirability of what could have been a simple loop handle.

£80–£120

Royal Worcester 1890
Height 9¼ins:23.5cm.
Printed crowned circle, registration, date code

A rather ugly jug, printed and coloured with an epiphyllum flower.

£25–£35

Royal Worcester 1892
Height 17½ins:44.5cm. Printed crowned circle, date code

A good ewer of Persian inspiration, having an ivory body with pale whip-lash floral enamelling. The neck and cover are pierced and the spout removable.

£500–£600

Royal Worcester 1894
Heights 5 and 7ins:12.8 and 17.7cm.
Printed crowned circle, registration, date code

Typical of numerous shapes of jugs or ewers produced by the factory in the last quarter of the 19th century and continuing the shapes well into the 20th. The decoration coloured and printed in gilding on apricot, shading to yellow, bodies.

£15–£20 each

Royal Worcester 1902
Height 9½ins:24cm. Printed crowned circle, date code

A very good little ewer with fine landscape painting by Harry Davis, signed. The rest of the body a clear apple green, making this a most desirable piece.

£200–£250

Royal Worcester 1907
Height 8½ins: 21.5cm. Printed crowned circle, date code

A well cast ewer with bronzed borders and a scene of sheep by Harry Davis, signed. Davis was known for his sheep, which fetch high prices. His less common landscapes, see p.147, are painted with greater care but are not much more expensive.

£100–£150

Royal Worcester 1915
Height 12¼ins:31.1cm. Printed crowned circle, date code

A pair of ewers of extreme ugliness, the pierced spouts and over-ornate handles doing nothing to help. The paintings by John Stinton, signed, are of his usual standard and his usual Highland cattle.

£350–£400

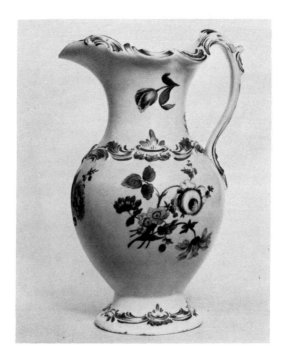

Unattributed c.1840
Height 13ins:33cm. No mark

An attractive ewer, well printed and painted with flowers, but not a collectable item. Originally made with matching basin for use as a washing set in bedrooms before plumbing. In the early 19th century these sets were often of good quality for use by the gentlemen and ladies of the household, but by the middle of the century the gentry were usually 'on tap' and only poor quality sets were made for the use of the servants in their garret rooms. They can be found as late as the first world war. Although very good for floral arrangements the ewers are still poor sellers.

£20–£25

Unattributed mid-19th century
Height 6¾ins:17cm. No mark

A large and decorative tankard transfer-printed with a puce outline and brightly enamelled design of a highly degenerate but amusing variation of the 18th century quail pattern originally itself based on the Chinese. The ground is also reminiscent of the *Companie-des-Indes* porcelain exported to this country from Canton.

£30–£40

Jugs, Mugs and Ewers

Unattributed c.1850
Height 7¾ins:19.7cm. Moulded registration

A well known parian jug with a cleverly thought-out answer to the handle problem, usually a dissatisfactory element in the design of these jugs. This example is cast in self-colour sage green, but can be found in other pastel tones or white. It is also known in stoneware at roughly the same price, or crude pottery and worth only £1—£2. The scene, entitled "The Gamekeeper" was issued in biscuit and porcelain by Minton and it is possible that this jug is also from the factory although the standard is not as high as usual.

£5—£10

Unattributed c.1858
Height 5⅛ ins:13.4cm. Moulded registration

A parian jug with the attractive decoration well set off by the coloured ground which has, in this case, been well applied and fired. The exterior has a matt finish whilst the interior is glazed.

£8–£12

Miscellaneous

This section includes all those wares that do not fit happily into larger groups and do not warrant a whole section to themselves, mainly because as a form they are not common.

ENAMELS

Enamels are used to obtain the colours on top of the glaze and are in simple terms finely ground coloured glass. This melts on firing and fixes itself to the glaze. Where it has started to flake off, the firing has failed to reach a high enough temperature to create a good fusing of enamel and glaze, or there has been a bad match in the coefficient of expansion of the two, so that over the years the constant rising and falling of room temperature has resulted in the enamel crazing and losing cohesion. Over-firing, on the other hand, can result in the warping of the piece or the burning of one or more of the colours.

GOLD

Gold for gilding is pure 24 carat gold in solution and can be applied like paint with a brush or printed and transferred. This standard is used for the best work, raised designs for example. For ordinary wares, 22 carat is employed and down to 10 or 12 carat proprietary brands are used for lustres. Different golds will produce different colours of gilding and very slight impurities of copper or other metals create other shades. Do not be fooled, as many people are, into believing that, when a piece they are buying has 'been decorated with pure 24 carat gold', it is something special. Even mass-produced every day services with gilding used pure or almost pure gold or the pattern would degrade during or after firing. 'Silver' is produced from platinum; rhodium is occasionally employed for different textures. The 'jewels' on pieces such as p.33 are blobs of enamel and much the same is used for 'simulated' jewellery.

PARIAN

Parian was the name given to a particular, hard, white porcelain body with an appearance of marble. Developed in the 1840s by a number of major manufacturers, including Copeland, Minton, Wedgwood and Worcester, it was also known as Statuary Porcelain. It was used mainly for reduced reproductions of famous marble statues by contemporary artists. There is some dispute over the actual discoverer, but it is certain that figures were being produced by 1844 by Copeland and Garratt. Large numbers of the figures were given away as prizes in lotteries, such as the Art Union, the Crystal Palace Art Union, etc.

The figures are mostly slip-cast and the 'signatures' that appear on them are those of the original sculptors and were part of the mould. Minton and Copeland figures both have date codes, others were often dated. The parian body was also employed for useful wares, including highly elaborate centrepieces and the frequently encountered jugs. It was also the material that enabled the English pâte-sur-pâte developed by M.L. Solon (p.409) to be so superior to its Continental hardpaste counterpart.

It is worth digressing a little into the method of producing most figures. This was by a technique known as slip-casting, used not only for figures, but also for moulded vases and jugs. From the original artist's model a plaster mould was produced, in two parts only for a simple jug, or sub-divided still further for more complex objects. Handles, high-relief heads and limbs, etc., were cast separately. The material for the body in the form of a liquid slip is poured into the mould to the brim and allowed to stand. The plaster absorbs the water from the slip, forming a film of clay on the inside of the mould. When the required thickness has been produced, the excess liquid is poured off and the mould containing the potential figure allowed to dry. The mould can then be carefully removed and the object, after the addition of any separate pieces such as handles which are stuck on with slip, allowed another drying before firing.

Miscellaneous

Belleek c.1870
Height 13¼ins:33.5cm. Early crest and Belleek

An early and rare candlestick with the boy in matt and the rest with a
shiny glaze, all well modelled. Pair £200–£300.

£70–£100

Belleek c.1895
Length 16¼ins:41.3cm. Printed symbol and names

A well decorated mirror frame, basket moulded and applied with sprays of lily-of-the-valley, their leaves in green. The flowers and leaves are very prone to damage.

£150–£200

Chamberlain & Co. c.1840
Width 12ins:30.5cm. Printed name

An extremely elaborate card tray with a well modelled and coloured border of shells and a scene of the (then) proposed Houses of Parliament which were in fact started in 1840 and finished in 1852.

£350–£500

Chamberlain and Co. c.1846
Length 7½ins:19cm. Printed name

A not uncommon model of King John's tomb in Worcester Cathedral. The exterior brightly enamelled and gilt and the top removable to reveal three inkwells and a pen tray. Without the wells which are frequently missing £80–£120.

£150–£200

Miscellaneous

Royal Crown Derby 1885
Diameter 17ins:43.2cm. Printed crowned monogram and date code

A very large and unusual revolving lazy Susan with an Imari pattern. Not only desirable from the point of a Derby collector but a good quality and usable object.

£100–£150

Grainger and Co. 1892
Diameter 6 $\frac{1}{8}$ ins: 15.5cm. Printed shield and date code

A good box and cover, double walled and pierced with scrolling picked out in gilding, the rim with turquoise beads. The slightly domed covers on these boxes are very prone to damage, making them uncommon in good state.

£150–£180

Miscellaneous

Grainger and Co. c.1900
Diameter 4½ins: 11cm. Printed shield

A box and cover with a blurry painting of a pheasant by James Stinton, the poor scroll-work gilt on an ivory-pink ground.

£35–£40

Minton c.1830
Height 10ins:25.4cm. No mark

An amazing piece of the porcelain flower makers' work and surviving in good condition, considering the fragility of the petals. The whole also brightly coloured. Although unmarked, the shape is known from the factory design books and like so much flower-encrusted ware would at one time have been attributed to Rockingham, a factory incapable of such elaborate work. Bad damage on a piece like this would result in a huge fall in price.

£450–£500

Rockingham 1826-1830
Diameter 4ins:10.7cm. Griffin in red and C1 3

A shallow pin tray with moulded rim. A gros-bleu border with gilt leaf meander and a central spray of coloured flowers.

£75–£100

Rockingham 1826-30
Height 1⅞ ins:4.8cm. Width 3¼in:8.2cm.
Griffin in red

A shell-shaped inkwell moulded in the form of a scallop with two shell feet and two shell penholders. Decorated with gilt scrolls and foliage. The complete item, which is much rarer, has both an ink pot and cover.

£40–£60 as shown. £60–£100 complete

Miscellaneous

Wedgwood 1920s
Diameter 2ins:5.1cm. Printed vase and name

An uncommon fairyland brooch with a polychrome and gilt pixie against a mottled beige ground. A similar sized brooch with a butterfly £30–£40. The mounts are of little consequence unless in gold and an unmounted example would fetch the same.

£140–£180

Worcester, Barr, Flight & Barr 1807-13
Length 6ins: 15.3cm. Printed name

An attractive inkstand of ingot form, well painted with a panel of garden flowers. The ends with gilt lyres and scrolls on a gros-bleu ground, the handle in the form of twisted dolphins. This example has only one of the two inkwells present. A complete example £180—£220.

£150—£200

Worcester, Flight, Barr and Barr c.1825
Diameter 9ins:23cm. Printed name

A card tray with overhead gilt handle springing from gilt leaves on the pale green ground. The central panel with a scene from the popular novel of the period Paul and Virginia. Subjects from the story are frequently found on English pottery and porcelain, pot lids, Staffordshire figures and even on continental wares and plaques.

£350–£450

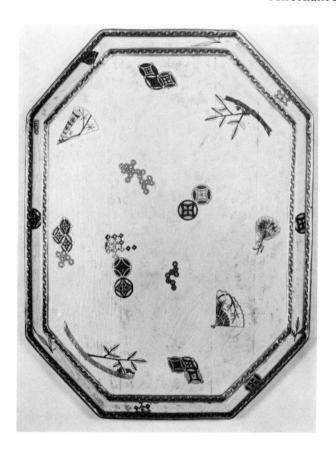

Royal Worcester c.1875
Length 17ins:43cm. Impressed crowned circle

An interesting tray with a Japanese-influenced design in bright enamels
and gilding on a simulated wood grain. Originally made for a tea service,
which would fetch £300–£400 complete.

£150–£180

Miscellaneous

Royal Worcester 1880
Height 13½ins:34cm. Printed crowned circle, date code

A bizarre candlestick in the form of a Japanese juggler, the colours in warm tones of bronze, dark brown and gilding on an ivory body. Candlesticks suffer most by being singles; they are always *much* better as pairs. Pair £400—£500.

£120—£150

Royal Worcester 1887
Height 8ins:20cm. Printed crowned circle, date code

Candlesticks are uncommon in Royal Worcester porcelain but not very desirable. This example in white relieved by gilt details. Pair £40–£60.

£10–£15

Miscellaneous

Royal Worcester 1897
Height 5¾ins:14.7cm. Printed crowned circle, date code

An interesting piece of absurdity in the form of a menu card simulating a battered fence on a tree stump. The 'Wild West' image spoilt by the usual apricot, peach and gilt coloration. Many different forms of menu card holders were made, and most would fetch these prices. Set of a usable eight £120–£180.

£10–£20

Royal Worcester 1901
Height 10ins:25.5cm. Printed crowned circle, date code

Not only are cheese dishes in little demand for use, but this one, despite being Worcester, is neither attractive nor well decorated.

£20–£30

Miscellaneous

Royal Worcester 1906
Height 3¼ins:8.2cm. Printed crowned circle, date code

A badly moulded posy-holder in white with a sage-green lily-leaf base. The overall effect is very dull, if not sinister, making this an undesirable and, quite properly, cheap object.

£8–£12

Royal Worcester 1921
Diameter 7¼ins:18.5cm. Printed crowned circle and date code

A late piece with printed outlines coloured and gilt on a peach ground. The spikes of the shell are obviously prone to damage and the small shell feet can become detached — so watch for restoration.

£30–£40

Royal Worcester 1930s
Height 3ins:7.5cm. Printed crowned circle, date code

A Toby jug loosely based on an eighteenth century original and made in a number of sizes, up to 6ins:15.2cm. £50–£70.

£15–£25

Royal Worcester 1974
Height 4ins:10cm. Printed crowned circle, date code

A candle snuffer in the form of a nun, companion to a monk. Both were made in the 1860s and continue in production today, the earlier examples up to £80.

£4–£6

Miscellaneous

Unattributed c.1825
Height 8½ins:21.5cm. No mark

A watch-holder in the form of a church tower, unusually sharply
modelled and well-painted and applied with flowers. The green base
gilt. These towers are also known in Staffordshire pottery and were
used to hold the owner's gold fob watch when he retired for the night.

£120—£180

Unattributed c.1840
Height 11½ins: 29.2cm. No mark

Although very well painted and gilt, door plates are not very saleable. Few people now have the right doors to screw them to, or are prepared to do so if they have and they are not large enough to display on their own. Even marked examples by Coalport or Copeland and Garrett are no more expensive.

£8–£12

Unattributed 1889 (hall mark)
Height $2\frac{1}{8}$ ins: 5.5cm. Registration

A silver-mounted scent bottle, datable from the mount. Not an identifiable factory, although at first glance it looks like Derby, but a persistent owner could trace the registerer of its design from the registration number, a long job, taking over two weeks.

£10–£20

Plaques

The ceramic painter in need of a canvas to display his ability turns to a flat slab of pottery or porcelain. These were made by the various factories mainly as convenient palettes for testing out new enamels or glazes and were only rarely produced as painted plaques on a regular basis by the factory. The artists employed frequently took the blanks home and worked on them after hours, although the materials and the firing were obviously supplied by the factory, probably with the manager's connivance. The finished plaques were then sold or given as presents by the artists. Other plaques were bought as blanks by outside decorators who worked in entirely private studios, their only contact with the factory being the final firing, although, judging from the poor standard generally, it would appear that some even undertook this themselves.

The slabs are frequently unmarked and it is dangerous to attribute them to a particular factory unless the artist is identified and his place of work known. Ceramic artists are, however, a traditionally itinerant lot, some managing to work for every major pottery in the Midlands before they died. Where a solid attribution is possible, a higher price is likely. Signed pieces are obviously better still. A named scene, an identified sitter of a portrait and a date are all aids to a good price. There was a vogue in the 1870s and 80s for ladies and other amateurs to take up painting plaques and plates on blanks supplied by leading factories. These are mostly earthenware but porcelain was employed and a full signature, a date and inscription in shaky script, a lack of factory mark and poor painting readily identifies these. They are not expensive. Amateurs also went in for painting in oils on porcelain. The results, again, are of practically no value. Oil paintings on sheets of milk white glass, which can be mistaken for porcelain by those unfamiliar with them, are *always* of vile quality.

A very few professional miniaturists, enamelists and portrait painters produced fine work on porcelain in the nineteenth century and these are collected and appreciated, as are the twentieth century plaques from Worcester and Aynsley.

Plaques

Possibly Minton c.1830
9¼ins. x 7½ins:23.5cm x 19cm. No mark

A well painted plaque painted by Steele who also worked for a number of other factories in the first half of the 19th century. Pair £500–£700.

£200–£300

Possibly Coalport c.1880
8¼ins. x 10ins:21cm x 26cm. **No mark**

A quite well executed plaque after a painting by Birket Foster. Landscapes are good subjects and reach better prices than anonymous portraits, as with paintings. Pair £900–£1,200.

£350–£450

Plaques

Copeland 1860–1870
Diameter 16ins:41cm. No mark

A good plaque painted by C.F. Hürten, signed, with pink and yellow roses beside an ivy-grown wall. Hürten was one of the best floral painters of the period. See also the vases on pages 368 and 369 Originally a set of four plaques illustrative of the seasons £1,500–£1,800.

£250–£300

Copeland c.1875
Length 27¾ins:70.5cm. Impressed name

A well painted plaque painted by Lucien Besche, signed. Besche was, like so many ceramic artists of the time, French. He started at Minton's before joining Copeland around 1872, and later turned to oils and ballet design. His ceramic painting technique is a series of meticulous strokes to build up the design which is usually not original, but a copy from a well known master, often Boucher or Watteau.

£350–£400

Plaques

Derby 1877
Diameter 15¼ins:38.6cm. No mark

Derby plaques are rare and this example is particularly well painted by the popular artist, J. Rouse. This is of the Royal Pets after Landseer and is signed and dated 1877.

£350–£450

Derby Crown Porcelain Company c.1880
Height 17½ins:44.5cm. Printed monogram

A well painted plaque by G. Landgraf, signed. The background is in white with a damask design of leaves and berries which is too subtle to show in the reproduction. Landgraf worked at Brown-Westhead, Moore's factory until 1880 when he moved to Derby, staying only three years. His work is rare, of high quality and very collectable.

£900–£1,200

Plaques

Possibly Minton c.1830-1840
7¾ins. x 9¾ins:18.5cm x 24.8cm. No mark

An attractive and brightly coloured bunch of flowers possibly painted by Thomas Tatler.

£100–£150

Minton 1841
4¾ins. x 3½ins: 12cm x 9cm

A good documentary plaque by John Simpson inscribed on the reverse: Mrs. William Keary, painted by John Simpson, Stoke upon Trent, 1841. The quality of Simpson's work is high and recognisable but the inscription is what makes the plaque particularly saleable; without it £60—£80. J. Simpson was the son of a Derby painter where he was first employed, working for Minton's from 1830—1847.

£300—£400

Plaques

Minton(s) 1865–1885
5ins. x 8ins:12.7cm x 20.3cm. No mark

A named view of Stokesay Castle in Derbyshire, painted by J. Evans, signed.

£40–£60

Mintons c.1885
7ins. x 10in:17.8cm x 25.4cm. No mark

One of Solon's suffering putti subjects, five of them caged and chained with a young woman floating amongst them, all in white on an olive-green slab. A well executed plaque and with more happening than with most. Compare with following example.

£400–£500

Plaques

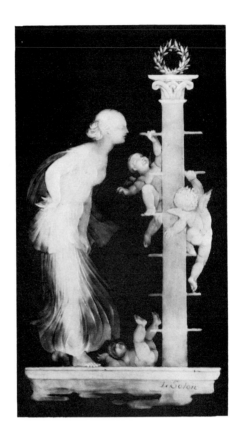

Mintons 1904–1913
8¼ins. x 4½ins:21.5cm x 11.5cm. No mark

A pâte-sur-pâte plaque by M.L.Solon with 'The Ladder to Glory' in white on a green-blue ground. The more usual type of Solon plaque with the background left black, the figures floating in space.

£150–£180

Wedgwood 1920s
Diameter 12¼ins:31cm. Printed vase and name

A large wall plaque with a bold Fairyland design. The reverse has, apart from the standard mark, an H in a chrysanthemum scroll, at present unexplained.

£600–£800

Plaques

Wedgwood 1920s
10¾ins. x 7¾ins: 27.6cm x 21cm. Printed vase and name

A fine Wedgwood plaque incorporating the signature of Daisy Makeig-Jones. The brilliant colours and gilding are well registered, making this amongst the most desirable of Fairyland items. Rectangular Fairyland plaques are, at present, unpredictable in price.

£800—£2,000

Royal Worcester c.1870
8¼ins. x 9½ins:20.6cm x 25cm. No mark

Painted by R.F.Perling, signed, after the original by Sir Edwin Landseer. Perling was a painter at Worcester from 1855 to 1885 and produced many plaques, many of them after Landseer. The companion plaque of the dying stag washed down a ravine with several hounds is a much less desirable subject, £60–£80.

£200–£250

Plaques

Royal Worcester 1903
10½ins. x 13¾ins:26.7cm x 35cm. No mark

An unusually large plaque of Windsor Castle by Harry Davis, signed
and dated. Typically this type of plaque has no factory mark, many
were done by the artists in out-of-work hours for themselves. A marked
piece would considerably increase the value, £500–£700.

£350–£400

Unattributed c.1830
Height 4¾ins:12cm. No mark

A fairly well painted plaque with a scene from Shakespeare's *Measure for Measure*. The technique of small blobs or streaks of colour to build up the design suggest that the painter was used to working on ivory and painting miniatures.

£25–£35

Plaques

Unattributed First half of the 19th century
8ins. x 7ins:20.5cm x 18cm. No mark

An anonymous gentleman, an anonymous factory and an anonymous
painter of little ability make this something of a ceramic non-event. A
large number of comparable plaques by almost amateur artists (note the
strange placing of the man's legs) were produced during the first half of
the 19th century.   Some manage at least charm, which make them
more expensive, or a Francis Bacon surrealism, which does not.

£6–£10

Unattributed 1855
6¾ins. x 5¼ins:17.5cm x 13.3cm. No mark

A portrait plaque of Marie Henriette, Duchess of Brabant, after the original by Sir William Ross and painted on porcelain by J. Simpson, signed, titled and dated 1855. The quality is high but the subject is far less attractive than Mrs. W. Keary, painted by Simpson, p.189, and is a copy of another artist's work, making this much less desirable.

£80–£150

Plaques

Unattributed 1859
14½ins. x 11ins:36.5cm x 28c. No mark

An exceptionally fine English plaque which is comparable with, if not better than, the majority of Continental examples. Painted by William B. Ford, signed and dated 1859, after the original oil by J.L. Dyckmans. Ford (1822–1896) was an enamellist on both copper and porcelain, this plaque having been exhibited at the Royal Academy in 1860. No other examples are known to have been sold recently.

£1,200–£1,500

Unattributed c.1870
16ins. x 11¾ins:40.5cm x 29.8cm. No mark

An anonymous but quite good plaque of a not unattractive subject.
Probably cheaper than the comparable subject on canvas.

£60—£80

Unattributed 1886
6½ins. x 11¼ins:16.5cm x 28.6cm. No mark

Painted by W. Wright, signed and dated 1886, and after the original painting 'Jack in Office' by Sir Edwin Landseer. In common with many of Landseer's works such as 'Death of the Stag' (see comment p.195), it has unfortunate overtones of blood sports, cloying sentimentality or in this case class discrimination which the buyer today is not prepared to tolerate. When the subject is transposed to porcelain it does not even have the advantage of being an original.

£80–£120

Plates, decorative and utilitarian

Plates have always been found a useful base for displays of artistic proficiency and have therefore been frequently used for decorative rather than utilitarian purposes.

Although single plates from rare or highly decorated eighteenth century services can justify a single lot at auction, only plates from a few special services or factories of the early nineteenth century warrant this treatment. Single plates otherwise are generally in the 50p to £5 region, unless they have been produced in fairly limited numbers, such as the Derby football plate (p.218). These were never intended for use, the plate being only a suitable canvas for the decoration.

Plates are nearly always press moulded by machine. A sheet of clay is stamped top and bottom into a mould, allowed to dry, cleaned up, glazed and fired. Mass production techniques have, to a greater or lesser degree, been in use since the beginning of the nineteenth century. Methods of decoration include the use of transfers, usually in one colour, as a basis for added coloration by hand, a technique still used and still cheaper and more efficient today than a machine. The design is sometimes 'tied together' after colouring by a further transfer in gilding from the same engraved plate as the first outline, as in Fairyland Lustre. Signed plates were entirely hand enamelled but executed to a fairly set formula.

Dessert as eaten during the nineteenth century has vanished from the dining table and with it the usefulness of the numerous services from which it was eaten. The result is that, unless of extremely high decorative quality suitable for filling a corner cabinet, they are very cheap.

Cauldon c.1900
Diameter 8½ins:21.7cm. Printed name, retailer's name

One of a set of sixteen game plates in a fitted box, each well painted with a different named bird or beast by J. Birbeck, signed. The rim royal blue with gilt scrolls. The set fetched £1,000 at auction because of their fine condition and decorative qualities. Cauldon produced little of such a high standard and there is no strong demand from collectors. The factory is therefore not a price factor and would be much the same for any other minor factory.

£30–£50

Chamberlain 1815-20
Diameter 8ins:20.2cm. Painted name

A very finely painted plate by Thomas Baxter and with a well-gilt border. The body highly translucent and known as 'Regent China'.

£300–£500

Plates, decorative and utilitarian

Coalport 1808 and 1809
Diameter 9½ins:24cm. No mark

Two extraordinarily rare plates, their interest lying in the fine painting by Thomas Baxter and in the fact that they are signed and dated by him. Only a few others are known. As can be seen in the photograph, they both have some wear to the wide gilt borders. A really immaculate example could fetch £800–£1,200.

£400–£600 each

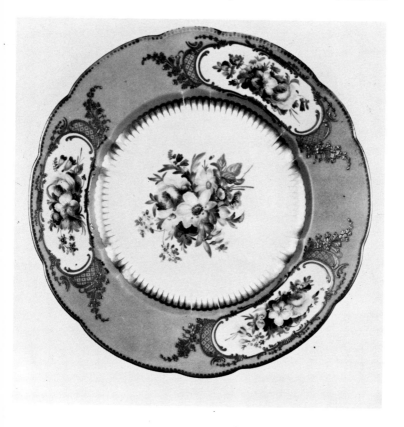

Coalport c.1850
Diameter 9½ins:24cm. Printed name

A well painted plate with panels on a gilt and pink border. Set of twelve
with four low and a high tazza, £200–£300.

£10–£15

Plates, decorative and utilitarian

Coalport 1861−65
Length 17¼ins:42.5cm. Painted name

The grey monochrome painting of Sarpedon borne by figures symbolic of Sleep and Death by R.F. Abraham. Red and gilt border. R.F. Abraham 1827-1895 worked at Coalport from 1850-1865 and was described in the Art Journal as the principal painter of the day. This dish would fetch more with a less mournful subject.

£150−£180

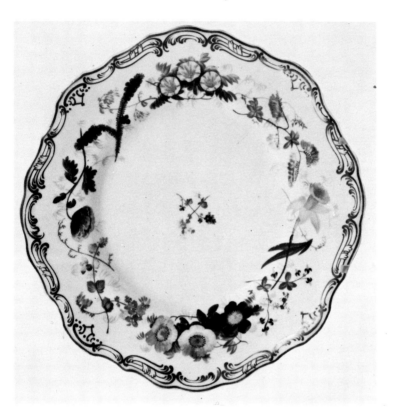

Copeland c.1860
Diameter 9ins:24cm. approx. Printed name

A gilt border enclosing a well painted border of bright summer flowers but let down by the sparsely decorated centre. Signs of wear on a plate of this type would reduce the price to £1–£2. Service of twelve plates, four shaped dishes and a tazza £80–£120. Had the centre been painted with a larger display £10–£12.

£5–£8

Plates, decorative and utilitarian

Copeland and Garrett c.1840
Diameter 9ins:23cm. Printed name

Typical of thousands of odd plates left over from services and now lurking unloved in antique shops all over the country. The wavy ribbon is a favourite motif from the 1830s to 50s. This example with hand coloured flowers over a puce outline against a lime green ground. The price given is for a perfect example, the one illustrated is worn, making it almost valueless. Service of twelve plates, tazza and four dishes, £40–£60.

£1–£2

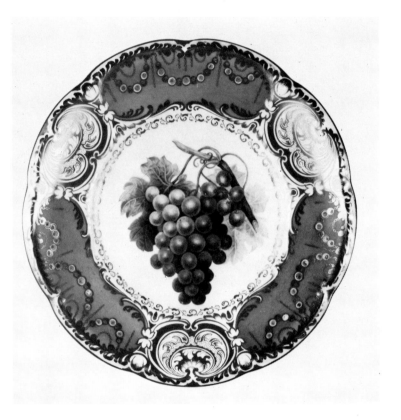

Davenport 1856
Diameter 9¾ins:24.8cm. Printed name, registration

An attractive and well painted plate from a service of two tall tazze, two low tazze and eight plates, each with a different named fruit, the border puce and gilt. Wear on a plate of this type is very disfiguring and can halve the price. Service as listed £150–£250.

£10–£15

Derby c.1810
Diameter 8 7/8 ins: 22.5cm. Painted mark

A finely painted pair of plates titled on the reverse A Wreck and In Italy, the borders in gilding with rich scrolls, the left plate worn at the bottom.

£180–£220 for pair

Royal Crown Derby 1878
Diameter approx. 8ins:22.2cm. Printed crowned monogram, date code

A rich, relief-gilt decoration in burnished gold and silver and with touches of enamel on an ivory ground combined with the Derby name makes this a desirable plate. The gold on these plates being both soft and in slight relief make it unlikely that they were ever intended for use; if they have been, the gilding is invariably scratched, reducing the price to perhaps £4–£6. Service of twelve plates, four low and one high stand £220–£250.

£10–£15

Derby Crown Porcelain Company 1884
Diameter approx. 9ins:24cm.
Impressed and printed monogram and crown, date code

An unusual plate from a dessert service, designed by John Joseph Brownsword who was Principal of Hull Art School, with transfer-printed scenes of children inspired by the book illustrator Kate Greenaway. The border claret. Service of twelve plates, four low and two high tazze £400–£500.

£15–£20

Derby 1891
Diameter 9¼ins:23.5cm.
Impressed name, printed monogram and crown including code

One of a well-known series of plates painted by James Rouse, senior, 1802-1888, signed on the reverse. The flowers in bright enamels and well painted. It is not recorded how many were painted and they turn up infrequently in the sale rooms. Rouse created a new style of flower painting and worked at all three Derby factories. His work is very desirable.

£250–£280

Plates, decorative and utilitarian

Royal Crown Derby 1893
Diameter 9ins:22.8cm.
Printed crown and cypher, registration and date code

A very rare and finely decorated plate painted by P. Taillandier, signed,
with a portrait within a candy-pink border. The rim pierced and gilt,
the whole extremely thinly potted and known as 'eggshell' porcelain.
Little is known about Taillandier except that he was the grandson of a
Sèvres painter, his work is very scarce, the only other example having
come on the market in recent years was in the same sale and was
painted with cupids and did not have the pierced border; it fetched
£300.

£400–£500

Royal Crown Derby 1913
Length 10½ins: 26.5cm. Printed monogram and crown with date code

An uninteresting dish, sparsely painted, with flower sprays within a dark blue and gilt rim. Service of four dishes and twelve plates £80–£120. Because of the lack of suitability for decoration due to the excess of white ground a service of this type is not very saleable.

£4–£5

Royal Crown Derby 1946
Diameter 10ins:25.4cm.
Impressed and printed monogram and crown, date code

An interesting commemorative plate for the 1946 Cup Final at Wembley with the Derby Coat of Arms and an inscription on the reverse. One of a limited number made for the players and officials and commemorating Derby's win.

£130–£150

Royal Doulton c.1910
Diameter 10½ins:26.6cm. Printed crown and lion

A good quality plate with gilt work in relief, the border pale pink. Doulton still produce plates of comparable quality.

£10–£15

Royal Doulton c.1910
Diameter 10¼ins: 26cm. Printed lion and crown

The flower panels by C. Hart, signed, within gilt and claret panels, the rim acid-etched. Royal Doulton was producing very fine porcelain at the turn of the century including non-functional plates such as this and the example on page 219.

£15–£20

Minton 1872
Diameter 9¾ins:24.8cm. Printed and impressed name, date code

A well painted plate by Henry Mitchell, signed with initials with a
pomeranian within a pierced gilt border and turquoise band.

£30–£40

Plates, decorative and utilitarian

Mintons 1874
Diameter 9½ins:24cm.
Printed crowned globe and impressed name with date code

A dessert plate well painted with fruit. The border in etched matt and burnished. Set of twelve plates, four high and four low tazze £350–£400.

£10–£15

Mintons 1878
Diameter $10\frac{1}{8}$ ins:25.7cm.
Impressed name and printed Paris Exhibition mark

A well-painted plate with a scene of French soldiers drilling on a quay within a brilliant turquoise border gilt with scrolls and oak leaves. A signature would add £10—£15.

£30—£50

Mintons 1880
Diameter 9½ins:24cm.
Gilt printed and impressed crown and globe, date code

A well painted plate by Marc Louis Solon, signed and dated 1880, with an unusual number of colours. The girl in sepia with cream-bordered drapery, chocolate scarf, pink hearts, pale blue thread, green cacti and an olive-blue ground, the border eau-de-nil and gilt. Apart from the large number of colours Solon did not execute many plates, making this a rare item.

£250–£300

Minton 1881-1882
Diameter 9½ins:24cm.
Impressed Minton, retailer's mark and date codes

One from a set of nine plates which fetched £600 at auction. Each well painted by Anton Boullemier, signed, with a different girl in contemporary costume in various settings, the rim gilt. This type of decoration with scenes which could be taken from popular novels of the period have only recently jumped the hurdle from being objectionably Victorian to being interestingly nineteenth century. Three years ago it is unlikely that the set would have fetched £100.

£30–£40

Plates, decorative and utilitarian

Minton 1888
Impressed name and date code,
printed Phillips of Oxford St. retailer's mark

A superb quality service to which the photograph could not do justice. A deep blue ground with very finely gilt leaves and flowers in grey and white. Price given for twelve plates, two low and one high tazza. As yet this type of highly refined service is not appreciated as it should be. Odd plate £5–£10.

£200–£250 (service)

Mintons c.1895
Diameter 9 ⅜ ins:23cm. Printed crowned globe

An unusual plate with white decoration on a black ground, the rim in salmon pink and gilding. Marc Louis Solon, who executed this dish, signed it, as always, L. Solon which has led to a great deal of confusion, as his son, who also worked as an artist for Minton in pâte-sur-pâte, although not of this type, was called Leon Solon. While in Paris where he started in pâte-sur-pâte M.L. Solon signed Miles, from his initials, such pieces being executed on hard paste porcelain.

£250–£350

Mintons c.1895
Diameter 9½ins:24cm.
Printed and impressed crown and globe, blurred date code

A fine plate in pâte-sur-pâte, but unsigned, with an amusing subject against a pale grey-blue ground. The impressed date codes of the late 19th and early 20th century on Minton pieces are often badly impressed, the series with a numeral inside a swan is particularly indecipherable.

£250–£300

Mintons c.1895
Diameter 10¼ins:26cm. Printed and impressed crown and globe

A pâte-sur-pâte plate by Alboine Birks, signed, with Venus and cupids against a pale blue ground. Well executed, but the scenes on too small a scale to be very exciting. The influence of the teaching of Solon on Birks is obvious in the subject matter chosen — cupids subjected to various minor tortures such as whipping, washing and roasting.

£80–£100

Mintons 1903
Diameter 8¾ins:22.2cm. Impressed name and date cypher

Painted by Leslie Johnson; signed, with a romantic girl in a garden. Vast numbers of plates with anonymous ladies languishing in interiors, gardens or landscapes are met with, usually from continental factories, but the English painters tried their hand also, rarely with the same success. A comparable continental subject might fetch in the £100–£200 region.

£35–£45

Moore 1892
Diameter 9ins:23cm. Printed name

An elaborately moulded plate looking suspiciously like Royal Worcester with printed gilding and coloured flowers. Service of a pair of tazze, two pairs of dishes and twelve plates £200–£250. Royal Worcester comparable service £300–£350.

£8–£10

Nantgarw 1813-22

Diameter 9½ins:24.1cm. Impressed name

A London-decorated Nantgarw plate with brightly enamelled birds in the centre. The border bright blue with gilt leaves.

£300–£350

Nantgarw 1813-22

Width 9½ins: 24cm. Impressed name

A superb dish from the celebrated service belonging to The Mackintosh of Mackintosh, chief of the Clan Chatton of Moy Hall, Inverness-shire. The service was decorated in London with different exotic birds within a flower-painted gilt border. Pieces of the service appear very infrequently on the market and are much sought after.

£800–£1,000

Nantgarw 1813-22

Diameter 9¾ins: 24.8cm. Impressed name

A brilliantly-decorated plate painted in a London studio with a vase of flowers, the border moulded with scrolls and painted with flowers and gilt details on a buff ground. The quality, rarity and sheer luxuriant exuberance makes this a very desirable plate.

£1,200–£1,400

Rockingham 1826-30
Diameter 11½ins:29.2cm. Printed griffin in red

A fairly standard Rockingham plate with moulded border and broad blue and yellow band gilt with trellis and leaves. The centre with a spray of flowers.

£30–£60

Rockingham 1826-30
Diameter 13ins:33cm. Printed griffin in red

A well painted dish with a wide gilt border containing bright exotic birds in a classical landscape. A rare and desirable example.

£150–£200

Rockingham 1826-30
Diameter 9½ins:24cm. Griffin in red

A gilt rim decorated with a deep green band with gilt ears of wheat and insects. The centre with a spray of pink roses. The item is typical of the lavish use of gilding in the early period of the factory.

£80–£100

Rockingham 1830-42
Diameter 9¼ins:23.5cm. Printed griffin in puce

Plates with C scroll moulding are of late date and quite common and were originally part of a service. A transfer-printed scene or mediocre flower-painting in the centre would command £20–£40. The high price of this example is accounted for by the finely painted scene. Worn gilding would reduce the price to £80–£120.

£140–£160

Swansea c.1815
Diameter 9ins:23cm. No mark

Hand coloured over a black print with the Mandarin pattern. A rare plate but not as collectable as a hand-painted plate.

£50–£70

Plates, decorative and utilitarian

Swansea early 19th century
Diameter 9⅝ins:24.5cm. Impressed name

Despite a little wear to the gilding, a very desirable plate from the Marquess of Exeter service. An identical service, which belonged to the Morell family at Gosforth Castle, did not have the impressed mark. This would not, in this case, have any effect on the price, as the provenance is so well established.

£200–£250

Wedgwood 1812—22
Diameter 8½ins:22.5cm. Printed name

A bone china plate transfer-printed and coloured with sprays of flowers in botanical style, the rim gilt and fluted. An interesting plate for a collector but the sprays of flowers not of the best and unhappily placed on the plate. Set of twelve plates and two tazze £180—£220.

£8—£12

Wedgwood 1908–12
Printed name

A twenty piece dessert service specially commissioned for the yacht of Herbrand, 11th Duke of Bedford and painted by J.P. Thornley, signed, with classical putti beneath the crest. This is the only service of this pattern but comparable services would fetch about the same.

£500–£600 (service)

Wedgwood c.1920
Diameter 9ins:23cm. Printed vase and name

Gilt printed scene on a powder-blue ground. A very dull production and not even popular with Wedgwood collectors.

£2–£4

Plates, decorative and utilitarian

Wedgwood 1920s
Diameter 10½ins:26.8cm. Printed vase and name

Although all fairyland plates are uncommon, this pattern with pixies crossing a bridge is the most frequently seen. The border of gilt fairies and flowers on an apricot band is typical. The underside is usually a mottled single colour, mauve, blue or pearl, rarely with further gilding. A plate with the identical pattern but much brighter coloration and better gilding £350–£450.

£220–£280

Wedgwood 1920s
Diameter 10⅝ins:27cm. Printed vase in gilding

The centre with pixies against a red ground, the rim with white and blue flowers on a black ground. Not a common pattern.

£300–£350

Wedgwood 1920s
Diameter 13¾ins: 33.5cm. Gilt-printed vase

An unusually large and well registered fairyland dish of particularly brilliant colouring. The underside mottled blue. The same dish but 'out of focus' — the gilding not in line with the colouring £350—£450.

£500—£550

Worcester, Flight, Barr and Barr c.1815
Diameter 8ins:20.3cm. Printed name

A brightly decorated plate with a so-called 'Japan' pattern. The price for a rubbed example, £30–£60.

£100–£150

Plates, decorative and utilitarian

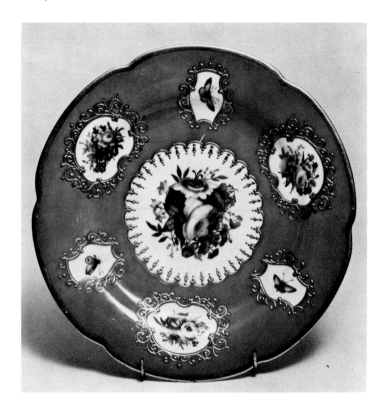

Worcester, Flight, Barr and Barr c.1825
Diameter 9ins:23cm. Printed name

A green ground plate with finely painted flowers and insects by Henry Stinton within gilt scrolls. Plates with these raised gilt scrolls are rarely found in pristine condition, resulting in a high price when they do. Note the passion flower, much beloved up to the middle of the century, after which time it is uncommonly found on porcelain, giving one a rough date guide.

£100–£200

Worcester, Flight, Barr and Barr c.1825
Diameter 9ins:23cm. Painted name

A green ground plate with gilt rim and border enclosing a dog rose study. Less well painted than the previous plate and with a less attractive but more modern layout. A transition from the small panels round the centre as found in the eighteenth century to the Victorian central bold spray or landscape.

£60–£80

Worcester, Flight, Barr and Barr c.1830
Diameter 10ins:25.5cm. Printed name

Odd survivals from armorial services such as this are not uncommon and when found are usually scratched or worn. The elaborateness of the arms affects the price considerably: an elaborate arms from a good family would fetch more than the price given and a plate with a crest only is worth £5–£10. This example with green border.

£80–£120

Worcester, Flight, Barr and Barr c.1830
Diameter 7½ins:19cm. Printed name

A version of a plate first made in the eighteenth century and known as
the 'Blind Earl' pattern. It was also made by Chamberlain's and Royal
Worcester. It is still in production.

£100–£200

Plates, decorative and utilitarian

Royal Worcester 1868

Diameter 9½ins:24cm. Impressed and printed crowned circle, date code

A well painted plate with a view, named on the reverse, one from a dessert service of twelve all with various English and Scottish views, the rims pierced and gilt on a turquoise band. Set of twelve with four tazze £350–£380. Set of twelve plates only £200–£250.

£15–£20

Royal Worcester 1890
Diameter 9½ins:24cm. Printed crowned circle, date code

A decorative plate with pierced rim in simulated stained ivory colours.
The centre painted by William Hawkins, signed.

£200–£300

Royal Worcester 1891
Diameter 9¼ins:23.5cm. Printed crowned circle, date code

A very run-of-the-mill shell dish with printed gilding and coloured flowers on an ivory ground.

£20–£30

Royal Worcester 1897
Diameter 8¾ins: 22.2cm. Printed crowned circle, date code

Decorated with pink orchids, green leaves and plenty of gilding, the rim bronzed. The shape can be found with birds by Baldwyn or cattle by Stinton, etc. These could rise to £40—£80 a plate.

£25—£35

Royal Worcester 1904
Diameter 10¼ins:26cm.
Printed crowned circle, date code, retailer's mark

A moulded and gilt rim, dark green border with flower sprays, a bouquet of summer flowers in the centre. Service of twelve plates, two pairs of shaped dishes and a tazza £400–£450.

£15–£20

Royal Worcester 1907
Length 10¾ins:27.3cm.
Printed crowned circle, Hadley monogram, date code

The decoration on this dish is after William Powell and bears his signature. Remember that Worcester artists often sign their work even when colouring over a transfer print, as this example, giving the impression of entirely hand-painted work. Although peacocks are considered unlucky by gipsies and country people, there are enough unsuperstitious buyers to support the prices without them. From a set of dishes, but decorative on its own. Set of twelve and four tazze £400—£600.

£35—£45

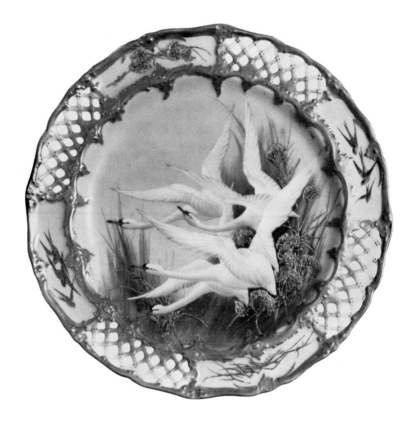

Royal Worcester 1908
Diameter 8½ins:21.6cm. Printed crowned circle, date code

Pierced rim and painted in the centre by C. Baldwyn, signed, with his typical swans against a blue sky. The foreground with raised gilt water plants. Baldwyn has a great following amongst Worcester collectors, possibly because there is little of his work about and a representative collection should obviously contain one piece of his.

£70–£100

Royal Worcester 1911
Width 9ins:24cm. Printed crowned circle, date code

Painted by J. Stinton, signed, with typical misty cattle scene. The border in deep blue and acid etched gilding. Service of twelve plates, two square dishes, two oval dishes and a fruit stand £700–£950.

£40–£60

Plates, decorative and utilitarian

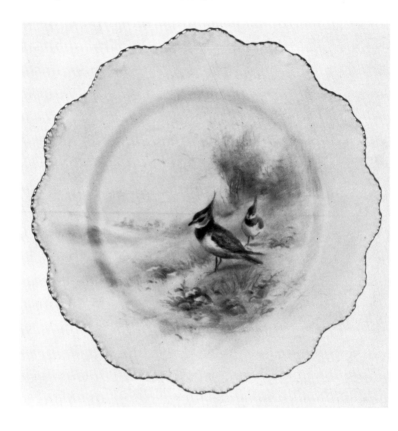

Royal Worcester 1912–14
Printed crowned circle, date code

A dessert service comprising a tazza, two pair of dishes and twelve plates, each painted rather weakly with a different game bird by James Stinton, signed. The moulded rim gilt. Single plate £15–£25.

£500–£800 (service)

Royal Worcester 1918
Diameter 9½ins:24cm. approx. Printed crowned circle, date code

A well-painted plate by A. Shuck, signed, with fruit within a gilt border of pink panels on a blue ground. Dessert service of two pairs of dishes and twelve plates £1,500–£2,000. The high quality and obvious richness of this set makes it highly desirable to collectors and for display.

£50–£70

Plates, decorative and utilitarian

Royal Worcester 1926
Width 8¼ins:20.9cm. Printed crowned circle and date code

A definite period piece of a type which needs greater recognition. The 20s and 30s style figures (see p.111) and painting on Royal Worcester are much too cheap for their scarcity and quality. This romantic scene of a girl in an Italian landscape is by Sedgley, and signed. Should rise in price fairly soon.

£15–£20

Royal Worcester 1939
Diameter 9¼ins:23.5cm. Printed crowned circle, date code

Painted by R. Sebright, signed, with rich fruit, the border of gilt scrolls on a powder-blue ground. Fine quality plates with fruit by Sebright or Shuck are rising fast in price.

£50–£100

Plates, decorative and utilitarian

Unattributed c.1870
Diameter 9ins:24cm. approx. No mark

Although at first sight quite attractive and of good quality, the painting
of the flowers leaves a lot to be desired. The pink ribbon, which has a
transferred outline runs from gilt pierced quatrafoils and results in the
whole having a somewhat anaemic look. Twelve plates and four tazze
£80–£120.

£4–£6

Unattributed c.1880
Diameter 9½ins:23.2cm. Impressed blurred name

Painted by W. Jones, signed, probably on a Continental blank. Quite decorative but the lack of a definite attribution makes these somewhat undesirable.

£20–£30

Plates, decorative and utilitarian

Unattributed c.1882
Diameter 8¾ins:21.3cm. Painted mark

An interesting plate painted by James C. Callowhill, a Worcester artist who in 1882 emigrated to America with his brother. This unmarked and presumably American plate is covered with a rich blue glaze decorated with gilt tooling and touches of pink and green enamels. Although rare it is less desirable than if it had been on a marked Royal Worcester body, then fetching £20–£30.

£15–£20

Pot-Pourri and Pastille Burners

As late as the middle of the nineteenth century, open sewers were still running through London and in 'The Great Stink' of 1858, Parliament was obliged to rise, due to the smell from the Thames, which was practically a flood of untreated effluent. There was a certain amount of skill involved when building a house for the wealthy to ensure that the household waste could be flushed conveniently away into a nearby stream, while at the same time siting the main rooms so that the smell was wafted away from the front. A change in the wind direction or a long hot spell, however, would give high living a new, and less attractive, flavour. To counteract this, the middle and upper classes burned incense in pastille burners or opened the lids of their pot-pourri to let out heavier and more pleasant aromas. They also carried small silver boxes with pierced inner lids containing a sponge soaked in pungent liquid for use in their carriages or out walking. All these were in real, practical use up to the 1870s when sewerage systems began to cope satisfactorily.

The idea of having a smell of flowers in a room, especially in the winter, continued to be attractive and still does today, so that the pair of pot-pourri (Worcester, p.278) were by no means anachronistic throwbacks. Rose bowls were not, as many seem to think, bowls for displaying cut blooms, but for rose petals, dried to retain their perfume.

Burning pastilles is an Oriental habit which still continues, joss-sticks now being most favoured. Originally, a small pellet of inflammable incense was burned on a convenient surface, a saucer sufficed, sending out clouds of rich perfume. It was obviously a great deal more amusing to place a pellet in a miniature house and have it issue from the chimneys, although it invariably leaked through the windows and door as well. The best examples are in two sections, the base having a small indentation for the pellet (p.287). Other more common examples simply have a hole at the back for the pastille. The style of building often reflects the interest of the time with Neo-Gothic follies, dinky flowered country cottages or Georgian mansions.

Pot-Pourri, Pastille Burners

Brown-Westhead, Moore and Co. c.1890
Height 20½ins:52cm. Incised

A good pair of vases from an infrequently met-with factory in the fine porcelain field, although they did exhibit often, with much praise, through the second half of the century. The decoration is in thick gold, silver and black against a rose ground, the neck pierced for pot-pourri. The paste from this factory is very soft, prone to fine crazing and discoloration, although these particular vases show little sign of this.

£300—£500

Grainger & Co. circa 1840
Height 4ins:10cm. Script name

A rare miniature pot-pourri basket and cover. Well painted with a named view of Spetchley House on a yellow ground, gilt with scrolls. The yellow ground makes all the difference, a blue example would fetch £80–£120.

£150–£200

Pot-Pourri, Pastille Burners

Minton c.1835
Height 10ins:25.4cm. Painted name

An attractively painted pot-pourri with a named scene of Buildwas Abbey, Salop., on one side, a bouquet of flowers on the other, surrounded by encrusted flowers. The mark on the bottom is that of the Meissen factories, underglaze-blue crossed swords. At this date many English factories were using the mark although the objects were not copied. The flowers on this example pretty much nibbled. Perfect £150—£200.

£100—£120

Minton 1869
Height 13½ins:34.2cm. Impressed name and date code

A good pot-pourri, after a Sèvres original. The well-painted figure subjects in tooled gilt panels reserved on the turquoise-blue ground. The large size and obvious decorative qualities makes this a very desirable item. Pair £700–£900.

£300–£350

Rockingham 1830-42
Diameter base 3¾ins:10cm. Height 6¾ins:10cm. Marked Cl 2 in gilt

An unusual pastille burner with a small plate-like base with a slightly raised central pastille platform with a perforated bulbous cover. The base and cover painted with floral sprays and gilt details. Some specimens are also encrusted with flowers.

£80–£100

Rockingham 1830-42
Height 11ins:27.7cm. Griffin in puce

A pot-pourri vase of campana shape, standing on acanthus feet and decorated with a landscape on one side and fruit and flowers on the other, enclosed by applied flower heads in white.

£250–£300

Pot-Pourri, Pastille Burners

Rockingham 1830-42
Griffin in puce

A pair of pastille burners of no great quality in the form of a perforated Grecian urn on a drum base decorated with gilding and applied with crudely moulded coloured flowers. Complete burners of this type are very rare.

The pair £500—£600

Photograph courtesy — Phillips.

Rockingham 1830-42
Height 7½ins:19cm. Printed griffin in puce

A rare shape for Rockingham with well modelled flowers left in the white and with touches of gilding on the handles and feet. The scenes of a standard best described as naïve. Better painting of the same scenes could send these to £500–£800. Circular pot-pourri baskets occur in several sizes and are much less rare, £40–£120.

£400–£600

Pot-Pourri, Pastille Burners

Spode c.1825
Height 3ins:7.6cm. No mark

A miniature pot-pourri in the form of a basket and cover, the gros-bleu body painted with flowers on a gilt scale ground. Although unmarked, the pattern number 1166 is present which ties in with known specimens.

£40–£60

Worcester — Flight, Barr and Barr c.1825
Height 6½ins: 16.5cm. Painted name

An attractive night light and pastille burner in the form of a cottage detachable from the grassy base. The whole well painted in naturalistic colours.

£200–£300

Royal Worcester 1882
Height 14½ins:37cm. Printed crowned circle, date code

The leaves in low relief, dark coloured, contrast well against the basket-moulded ground. The lids cleverly designed so that by revolving them the pot-pourri bouquet is cut off.

£400–£500

Royal Worcester 1891

Heights 7½ and 10ins: 19.5 and 25cm. Printed name and date code

An unusual garniture painted with flowers. The knop on the central vase is in fact conical; it was truncated in the photograph. Sets such as this have nearly always become separated and rarely appear complete.

£350–£400

Pot-Pourri, Pastille Burners

Royal Worcester 1899
Height 4¾ins:12cm. Printed crowned circle, date code

A pot-pourri with pierced cover and inner lid, painted gilding and gilt-printed outline. Not very good quality but helped by the deep colours rather than the washed out variety and with thick gilding. Without inner lid £20—£30.

£30—£40

Royal Worcester 1905
Height 7¼ins:18.4cm. Printed crowned circle, date code

A Grainger shape painted by James Stinton, signed. The piercing not very well finished.

£200–£250

Pot-Pourri, Pastille Burners

Royal Worcester 1909
Height 8ins:20.3cm. Printed crowned circle, date code

A good pot-pourri with crisp moulding coloured in shades of pink, green and orange with gilding. Others of smaller size, more frequently found, are less desirable, as are those with the Gothic scrolling blurred

£100–£150

Royal Worcester 1924
Height 11½ins:29cm. Printed crowned circle, date code

A large and decorative pot-pourri and cover painted by J. Stinton, signed, the pierced neck in bronzes and golds. The swags on this quite common pattern of pot-pourri are particularly vulnerable to damage, and are often restored, as are the knops. With slight restoration £400–£450. It is interesting to realise that this shape is still made by Royal Worcester and a present day piece, fully decorated by hand with some such subject as fruit, would cost something like £600 which makes the price of earlier pieces cheap.

£600–£700

Pot-Pourri, Pastille Burners

Unattributed first quarter of the 19th century
Height 5¼ins: 13.2cm. No mark

A very rare arbour group of a boy under a lilac trellis encrusted with flowers and moss, the base with gilt line border. The lilac ground makes a great deal of difference here to the price as with pastille burners, see p.286 and 287. Other colours £60–£80. Pair as illustrated £150–£250.

£100–£150

Unattributed c.1825
Height 7ins:17.8cm. No mark

An amusing burner with green roof encrusted with flowers, the brown base with gilding and an arbour. The naïve quality of construction and childlike simplicity of the flower modelling make this a most desirable piece.

£200–£300

Pot-Pourri, Pastille Burners

Unattributed c.1830
Height 8¼ins:21cm. No mark

An amusing castle pastille burner coloured lilac and with coloured encrustation and gilding. The leaning tower is accidental, having occurred during firing, a thing the tree support on the right was supposed to have prevented, but here it merely adds to the charm of the piece. Other colours apart from lilac £70—£100.

£150—£200

Unattributed c.1835
Height 7¾ins:19.8cm. No mark

A pastille burner with a basic lilac ground applied with coloured flowers and gilt. Other colours than lilac £50–£80, plain white £35–£50.

£100–£150

Pot-Pourri, Pastille Burners

Unattributed c.1850
Height 4ins:10cm. No mark

A pastille burner of reasonably good quality, with small flowers on a lavender ground, making this fairly expensive. As can be seen in the photograph the lid is chipped, a perfect example £60–£100. Note that such burners are usually sold as Rockingham which they are not. There is no evidence to suggest that the factory ever used the shredded clay technique as evidenced on this piece or on the sheep and dogs, similarly wrongly attributed.

£40–£50 as shown

Table Wares & Dinner Services

This is a section devoted to the items which are used at table, with the exception of plates. The odds and ends of services that survived the violent hands of the under-the-stairs staff were often kept for decoration and the tureens and dishes occasionally appear on the market separately. Their value now lies in their appeal as decoration — the larger and more elaborate they are, the better. Coats of arms of recognised families are a plus factor whereas monograms and, to a lesser extent, crests, detract from the price.

Dinner services are a strange market and the prices they fetch need some explanation. Taking for example one of the thousands of ironstone services made by Mason and his imitators in the first half of the nineteenth century, one would find that an odd plate might fetch 50p. at an auction — suitable only for decoration. A set of a dozen plates would creep up to perhaps £1 a plate but no more since for use at table one needs all the tureens, vegetable dishes, side plates, etc. However, in services containing a dozen of everything, tureens, etc., the total number would be around one hundred items and the price could have jumped to £2—£3 a piece. The chance of someone coming across exactly the pattern for which he is looking in any one sale is extremely remote so that most services are bought by dealers who may have to hold them as stock for many years before a purchaser buys them. The result is that to avoid tying up too much capital they do not spend as much on a service as it should warrant.

Belleek c.1870
Height 13ins:33cm. Impressed name, retailer's mark

A pair of centrepieces from the service of a design ordered for the Prince of Wales, palely-coloured and nacreous-glazed. The prices of this service seem to be more unpredictable than most Belleek, identical pairs having fetched in one season between £150 and £1,200.

£300–£600

Belleek c.1880
Height 12¾ins:32.5cm. Printed symbol and name

A fine uncoloured centrepiece, the good nacreous glaze showing off the sharp casting to the full. Typical sea-life influence with the figures from sea mythology, a young Triton, a mermaid and a hippogryph.

£200–£250

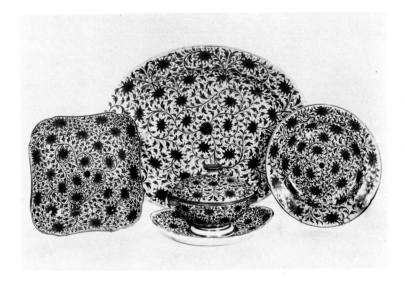

Coalport c.1825
No mark

A brightly decorated service of soup tureen and cover, two sauce tureens, covers and stands, nine meat dishes in sizes, fruit bowl, twenty-four dinner plates, ten soup plates and ten dessert plates, each painted with iron-red and gilt chrysanthemums. Single plates £8–£12. This is the type of service which could well be split by a dealer after purchase to sell as individual or pairs of plates, as they are very attractive in small doses, a whole service being, perhaps, a little overpowering.

£600–£800 the service

Coalport c.1830
No mark

A fine service of a fruit stand, two sauce tureens, covers and stands, four shell-shaped dishes, four lozenge-shaped dishes, two square dishes and eighteen plates. Each piece with a different landscape scene including figures within a bright gilt border. Single plates £15–£20. A variation in the border is known with the national emblems in gilding; this would raise the price to £25–£30 a plate.

£800–£1,000 the service

Coalport c.1860
No mark

A finely painted dessert service of twelve plates, two tall and four low stands, each with a different fruit within gilt and coloured border enclosing a crest of a squirrel. As with all stands on feet, watch for restoration or signs of gluing at the junctions of foot and dish. The piece was made in two parts and stuck with slip before firing and this remains a weak point; the glaze often settles in a crackled ring here and the clear adhesive is almost invisible.

£300–£350 the service

Davenport c.1805-15
Overall length 11¼ins:28.5cm. Longport in red script

Pierced dessert basket, painted with a Chinese garden scene in colourful enamels. Gilt twig handles. Early Davenport porcelain marked 'Longport' is quite rare.

Basket and stand £50–£80.   Basket alone £30–£50

Davenport c.1830–1840
Printed name

A good service of twelve soup plates, twenty-four dinner plates, twelve side plates, two sauce tureens and covers, two vegetable dishes and covers and nine meat plates, each piece well painted with sprays of flowers and with gilt border.

£300–£500 the service

Davenport c.1835
No mark

A fine botanical service with a different flower within scroll borders in blue and gilding. Comprising fruit stand, two sauce tureens, covers and stands, four oval dishes, four rectangular dishes and twenty-four plates. This works out at about £20–£25 each for a plate, to £50–£80 for a tureen. If the flowers were named the price could be half as much again.

£1,200–£1,500 the service

Davenport 1870–1886
Diameter 9½ins:24cm approx. Printed name

Davenport made both very high quality porcelain in the 1840s–1860s, often unmarked, and also mass produced wares for the lower end of the market. This continued to the end of the period but one meets less and less of the better items. Dessert service of a high tazza, two low tazze and twelve plates £200–£300.

£12–£15

Derby First quarter of the 19th century
Painted crossed baton and crown

A good quality service with an attractive design of coloured roses and garlands of cornflowers and gilt leaves, the 1796 pattern. Price for soup tureen and cover, two sauce tureens with covers and stands, two vegetable dishes and covers, seven meat dishes in sizes, twelve soup plates, twenty-four dinner plates.

£220–£300 the service

Royal Crown Derby 1882-95
Printed crowned monogram and date codes

A large composite service for dinner, dessert and tea: 12 soup plates, soup tureen and cover, 24 dinner plates, eight meat dishes in sizes, two sauce tureens, covers and stands, eighteen dessert plates, twelve pudding plates, twelve side plates, twelve cups and twelve saucers, two tazze, two lozenge dishes and two handled dishes. Large services of this type frequently have different date codes as the family added what they needed and included replacements. It is unlikely that another service would have the same composition as listed here but it does give a guide to a typical make-up.

£800–£1,000 the service

Derby Crown Porcelain Company 1890
Printed monogram, retailer's mark and date code

A muffin dish and cover from a service of twelve large plates, side plates, cups and saucers and two serving dishes. Each piece has pastel-coloured and gilt wild flowers, grasses and butterflies by John Porter Wale and the monogram CHS. It is this last which results in the low price of £100–£120 for the set. Collectors dislike anonymous monograms.

£3–£5

Hill Pottery, Burslem (S. Alcock) c.1840
No mark

A good quality service from an uncommon factory, which, despite the name, made some fine porcelain. The flowers in panels on a pink ground scattered with yellow flowers and gilt scrolls. Service of eighteen plates, three high and two low bowls, £450–£500.

Plate £10–£15; Bowl £20–£25

Minton c.1830
Height 14½ins: 37cm. No mark

A 'spot the deliberate error piece'. It is worth studying the proportions of this tureen, cover and stand as an object lesson to be on one's guard when buying. If it looks a little uncomfortable, read no further. What has happened is that the body originally had a foot which has parted company, the edge has been ground down and now rests fairly happily on the (intentionally) detachable base. Still a good quality and satisfactory object but liable to wild fluctuations in price, hence the wide quote.

£150–£300

Minton c.1840
Width 13½ins:34.4cm. Painted ermine mark

A turquoise-ground salver painted with two fighting stags in the centre. A large decorative item and therefore popular for display. Both Coalport and Minton achieved great success with the turquoise glaze they were using in imitation of Sèvres in the middle of the century, Minton's being less prone to black firing specks.

£100–£150

Minton 1851
Height 6½ins:16.5cm. Impressed name and date code

A clumsily-moulded figure holding a shell for uşe as a sweetmeat, or salt, uncoloured but for touches of celadon. Compare with the Worcester figure page 98. Pair with male £60–£80.

£30–£35

Minton 1870
Impressed name, printed retailer's mark, date code

A fine quality service but not decorative enough for display and the crest makes it less desirable for table use. The borders are in turquoise with matt and burnished gilding. Service of twelve soup, dinner and dessert plates, soup tureen, cover, stand, two vegetable tureens, covers and stands, sauce tureen, cover and stand and six meat dishes in sizes, £100–£200.

Tureen £5–£10; Dish £3–£5

Rockingham 1830-42
Griffin in puce

This type of C scroll moulding on the rims of plates and dishes is typical of late Rockingham but only by a careful study of the details of the scrolls can it be differentiated from the many other C scrolls of other factories. The part service comprising eight plates, one comport, two quatrefoil dishes and one tazza.

The service £400—£450

Photograph courtesy — Christie's.

Table Wares and Dinner Services

Swansea c.1815–1817
Impressed name

A fine service probably painted by D. Evans and in bright deep colours.

Pair of sauce tureens, covers, stands	*£600–£800*
Large centre dish	*£200–£300*
Other dishes	*£150–£200*
Plates	*£80–£120*

Swansea c.1820
Diameter 7ins:17.8cm. Red transfer name

A fine pierced fruit stand, the bowl and base both with cut lozenges and hoops, with fruit and flowers painted by David Evans and with good gilding. Altogether a rare and desirable piece.

£800–£1,200

Swansea Early 19th century
Diameter 7¾ins:18.5cm. No mark

An uncommon Swansea tureen of the same form as those illustrated in the service on page 308 on a pale green ground which adds considerably to the price. The scarcity of larger pieces from Swansea services generates much interest when they do appear on the market. It should be remembered that collectors display their collections in cabinets and need to break up rows of plates with more interesting shapes.

£600–£700

Worcester, Flight, Barr and Barr c.1820
Diameter 7½ins:19cm. Printed name

A sauce tureen, cover and stand with a rose within gilt scrolls on a green ground. Not a particularly exciting piece but the gilding is of good quality and green is a very saleable colour, blue ground £120–£150, yellow £250–£350.

£200–£300

Royal Worcester 1898
Printed crowned circle, registration, date code

A game service of twelve plates, a large meat dish, two small dishes and
a sauce tureen, cover and stand. Each piece with a printed outline,
brightly coloured and gilt, of a different game bird, the border sepia.
Despite the partial mass-production a well produced service, odd plates
£5–£10.

£250–£300 the service

Royal Worcester 1912
Printed crowned circle, date code

A typical mass-produced service of the period and comparable to similar services made today. Printed basic variation of the Indian tree pattern with hand colouring. Price for twelve soup plates, twelve fish plates, twelve side plates, twelve dinner plates, soup tureen, cover and stand, two vegetable tureens and covers, sauce tureen and cover and a gravy boat, six meat dishes in sizes.

£150–£200 the service

Unattributed 1850
Diameter 13ins:33cm. Registration of design

Badly cracked through the base. An interesting piece for the registration of design mark on the base for 1850, indicating the style of the period, and for the technique of well printed puce outlines for the well coloured flowers. A high quality production altogether. Perfect £70–£90.

£35–£45 (damaged)

Tea, Coffee Services

The damage problem that dinner services suffer from applies also to tea and coffee services — incomplete sets are of little use unless of a very fine quality and highly decorative. Since the teapot was the most complex article in a set and received the most use, it is most likely to be damaged or to be missing altogether. Teapots, in good condition, are scarce. The make-up of the service probably varied when it was bought, the customer ordering from a pattern book or samples, no doubt omitting the teapot if the family brewed in silver. The factories that employed date coding, when they made up orders, simply removed from stock shelves articles of the same pattern which might have been sitting there for a year or more, with the result that the codes vary. Again breakages could be replaced by quoting the pattern number but the replacement would have a later code. On usable services such as the Crown Derby Imari patterns this does not affect the value but on elaborately hand-painted sets which have not been properly matched, the price would be lowered. Since tea plates were unknown until the second half of the century many plates were made to match existing cups and saucers for services that were still in use at the introduction date, 1870-80. Well-painted boxed coffee sets, pages 347, 348 and 349, often with silver spoons, are a rising market, selling well to American buyers.

Belleek c.1870
Printed crest

Compare this with the cup and saucer on page 320. This example is of
the earlier period, crisply moulded and well coloured under a nacreous
glaze. Milk jug, sucrier or basin £7–£10; cake plate £2–£3. The teapot
is illustrated opposite.

£6–£8

Belleek c.1870
Width 8ins:20.4cm. Printed crest

Moulded and coloured grasses, all with a lustrous glaze. Belleek teapots are not uncommon, large numbers must have been sold separately from the rest of the service for decoration, a reversal of most factories.

£20–£25

Belleek 1872
Width 10¾ins:27.3cm. Printed crest and registration mark

A good piece from the first period, all well coloured and gilt. The use of sea motifs is the most obvious characteristic of Belleek, also the use of nacreous (shell-like iridescent) glaze. It can be found with an elaborate stand in the form of a dragon on four paw feet, £150—£250, but watch for matched-up sections of different dates.

£80—£120

Belleek c.1875
Width 9½ins:24.2cm. Printed crest and name

A teapot and cover of unusual design under an iridescent pearl-like glaze. All of good quality. A similar example with the more common shiny glaze £80–£120, coloured £150–£200. It is most important with Belleek that the mark should be the early dog, harp or tower and the name without the words 'County Fermanagh, Ireland' which indicates a date post 1891. Later pieces which look much the same can be a quarter the price.

£100–£150

Belleek c.1900
Late printed crest mark

A really badly moulded cup and saucer with wishy-washy pink-tinged rims and of the post 1891 period. Thinly cast with shiny glaze. Also found with green and gilt rims. Plate £0.50–£1; teapot £10–£12; milk jug or sucrier £4–£6; cake plate £2–£3 each.

£2–£3

E.J.D. Bodley 1876
Printed and impressed initials, registration

A cup and saucer from a minor factory which produced mainly useful wares. Thinly cast and moulded with sprigs of apple blossom coloured pink, gilt rim. Set of teapot and cover, sugar basin, milk jug, four cups and saucers and a tray £20–£25.

£0.50–£1.50

Copeland 1833–1847
Printed wreath and crown, titled in red

The reasonably well painted panels of English and Scottish views on this service are named on the bottom of each piece, adding a great deal of interest but not much value. The rest of the body with gilt scrolls on primrose yellow ground. Set of twelve coffee cups, twelve tea cups, twelve saucers, milk jug, two cake plates and a basin £120–£150; with teapot £150–£180.

£4–£6

Davenport c.1850
Printed name and registration

A superbly rich tea service in orange and gilding. Service of twelve cups, saucers and plates, milk jug, bowl and two cake plates £300–£350.

£10–£15

Tea, Coffee Services

Davenport 1870—1886
Printed and impressed name

Part of a service of eight cups, saucers and plates, two dishes, a bowl and a milk jug, each with iron-red, blue-green and gilt flowers. With teapot £90—£120.

£60—£70 the service

Davenport c.1880
Printed and impressed names, retailer's mark

Part of a service of six coffee cups and saucers, six tea cups and saucers, twelve plates and two cake plates. At first sight a Royal Crown Derby service in Imari style and in the same palette. Rarer than Crown Derby but less collected.

£200–£250 (service)

Bloor Derby 1825–1840
Printed circle mark

The shape of the milk jug or teapot or handle shape is nearly always the best give-away for an unmarked service. This set has the circular Bloor mark in red. Decorated in blue, iron-red and gilding. Comprising dish and cover, two pairs of dishes, bowl, milk jug, six egg cups, twelve breakfast cups, twelve tea cups, twelve plates and twelve saucers. It is worth pointing out that a comparable brand new service of this size could cost rather more.

£150–£250 the service

Royal Crown Derby 1899
Printed crowned monogram, date code

A superb quality service of the 'Brighton' shape made to order with a red, green and gilt monogram within a gilt 'rose pompadour' border. Cup and saucer £8–£10. A service of this kind would probably never have had a teapot, sucrier or milk jug, these would have been silver.

£150–£250 for twelve

Royal Crown Derby 1913
Printed crowned monogram, date code

A cabaret service of 'Dublin' shape comprising teapot, milk jug, sucrier, tray and four each cups, saucers and plates all with an Imari pattern number 2451. An additional two cups and saucers, bringing the total to a more usable six, £250–£300.

£220–£250

Royal Crown Derby 1922
Printed crowned monogram and date code

The famous Derby Imari pattern known to the cognoscenti as 1128 from the pattern number, not to be confused with the similar 2451 on the previous page. A service of twelve plates, cups and saucers, bowl, milk jug and two dishes about £300–£400. The actual date of manufacture matters little as long as it is post 1890, when the quality improved.

£300–£400 the service

Probably Coalport c.1810
No mark

An attractively refined service of neo-classical form with a band of green and gilt oeil-de-perdrix. Price for teapot, cover and stand, sucrier and cover, milk jug, six cups and six saucers.

£80–£120 the service

New Hall c.1810
Pattern numbers

The borders in neo-classical style with gilt leaves berried in iron-red. Price for teapot, cover and stand, sucrier and cover, milk jug, two saucer dishes, a bowl and eight cups and eight saucers.

£120–£140 the service

Rockingham 1826-30

A cup and saucer with moulded overlapping primrose leaves crudely coloured in yellow shading to green with gilt veins. Can be found with red mark or puce griffin and even when unmarked, as is not infrequent, can be positively attributed to factory, since no other used this mould.

£40–£50 unmarked. £50–£60 marked.

Rockingham 1826-30
Griffin mark in red and 599

This shape appears unique to the Rockingham factory, the saucer having a very deep foot rim and the cup handle not having a precise counterpart in any other factory. The appearance of the floral bouquets on interiors only give a dull impression with a resulting low price.

£20–£40

Rockingham 1826-30
Griffin in red and 684

A stylish Empire design with gilt bands that would not shame the 1930's art deco period. The shape is very rare. The handles are in the form of a horse's hoof with the upper portion representing a tail, which in a tea service is unique to the factory, no mark being necessary to provide attribution.

Trio as shown, £60—£70

Rockingham 1826-42
Griffin mark in puce and 612

Although this shape of cup and saucer is typical of the teaware produced by Rockingham in the early period 1826-30, it was also made post 1830. It is virtually identical in mould with a Ridgway production and unmarked samples are difficult to attribute. This example is decorated with gilt scrolls and foliage on a gros-bleu ground, the larger leaves in apricot.

£25–£35

Rockingham 1830-42
Printed griffin in puce

A late service, each piece in grey, outlined in gilding and with strawberries. Note the typical Rockingham crown knops. Service as shown with twelve tea cups, twelve coffee cups and twelve saucers and a basin.

£200—£300 the service

Rockingham c.1835
Width 8ins:20.4cm. No mark

The crown knop is typical of post 1830 Rockingham but the flamboyant grey and gilt scrolls can be found on many factories of the period. Desirably there should also be a stand in the form of a plate with a depressed well. Neither stand nor pot is ever marked. Perfect example £30–£60. Similar teapot but not Rockingham, damaged £5–£10; perfect £15–£25.

£15–£25 as shown

Rockingham 1835–1840
Printed griffin

Well-painted roses in pink with gilt lining.

Cup £20–£30; plate £25–£35

Spode c.1810
Painted name

An extremely rare set of tulip cups on a Spode pottery tray. All brightly coloured with coloured or gilt bases. A single cup £80–£100. A perfectly matched set, since these cups do not all have the same decoration, £1,000–£1,200.

£800–£1,000

339

Swansea c.1815–1817
Impressed name

Painted by Pollard. A complete service would actually be extremely rare, one is much more likely to see the pieces sold separately as examples. Cup and saucer £30–£40; teapot £100–£150; other pieces £40–£80.

£600–£800 as illustrated with twelve cups

Swansea c.1820
Impressed name

A superb Swansea Cabaret set as illustrated. Each piece painted in London with various growing flowers and with gilt borders. All in Empire style. The Empire style was rarely reflected in porcelain in this country to so great an extent as displayed here. A single teapot would fetch about £150–£250.

£1,200–£2,000

Wedgwood c.1815
Red stencilled name

Bone china cup and saucer, quite rare. Green cell diaper with printed figures, hand-coloured on top.

£20–£40

Wedgwood 1878–1891
Width 5ins:12.8cm. Printed name

A rare teapot of a design harking back to neo-classicism. The medallion bronzed and gilt, all of fine quality and very desirable for a Wedgwood collector.

£80–£120

Worcester, Barr, Flight and Barr c.1810
Printed name

A Barr, Flight and Barr set of tea cup, coffee can and saucer, each piece finely painted by Samuel Smith with shells on a simulated marble ground. Odd cup £30–£50.

£200–£300

Royal Worcester 1881
Printed crowned circle, date code

A reasonably well painted service with coloured flowers, and a good buy for use, the sum total probably being less than the parts and considerably less than a comparable modern service. Teapot and cover, milk jug, basin, two cake plates and twelve cups, saucers and plates £160–£180.

Teapot £25–£35; plate £2–£3

345

Royal Worcester 1890
Height 9¾ins:24.8cm. Printed crowned circle with date code

Not a particularly attractive coffee pot with ugly cover not helped by weak gilding and thin enamels on the ivory-coloured body. A service of twelve cups and saucers, cream jug, sucrier and coffee pot £200–£300.

£30–£40

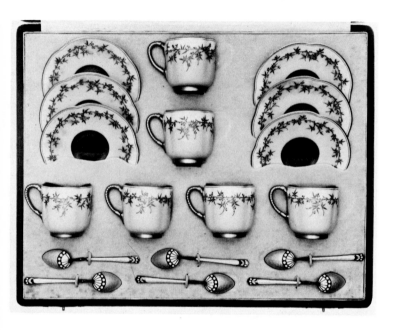

Royal Worcester 1912–1913
Printed crowned circle, date code

The mouth of each cup with a yellow band edged with raised gilt leaves, the interior of the cup as is usual, burnished gilt. The rather dull decoration of this set is helped by the art deco enamelled silver spoons which bear an import mark, indicating that they were made abroad. There is no need to worry about slight discrepancies in date codes on any sets of Royal Worcester or Crown Derby. The sets were made up from shelf stock and pieces might well not get used for a year or two.

£100–£150

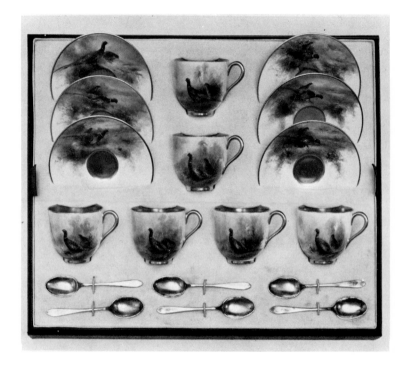

Royal Worcester 1928
Printed crowned circle, date code

A boxed coffee service with silver spoons painted by James Stinton, signed, with pheasants, the interiors of the cups gilt. These sets are now very popular and can be found with fruit £250–£300 or Highland cattle £250–£350.

£300–£350

Royal Worcester 1929
Printed crowned circle, date code

An uncommon form of decoration by Jack Stanley of hunting scenes. Much rarer than the Stintons' work or fruit subjects, but fetching no more because the former are more desirable.

£300–£500

Tea, Coffee Services

a   b   c   d

Royal Worcester Various dates
Printed crowned circle, date codes

An interesting comparison of single cups and saucers, ignoring the spoons. a. Fruit by Townsend, signed, 1934, £20–£30. b. Powder-blue ground, gilt border, 1926, £5–£10. c. Pheasants by James Stinton, signed, 1927, £25–£35. d. Transfer-printed roses, gilt-edged green scroll border, pierced silver mounts, 1905, £3–£5.

Vases

Vases were usually made purely for decoration and not to hold flowers. The price is now governed by the quality and decorative value, and, as always, by the factory. There are quirks in this section as in the others. The Minton flower-encrusted vase (p.397) was really quite cheap, because the heavy flower encrustation put off buyers who feared damage and because of the impossibility of cleaning it.

Watch out for vases that have lost their covers; these are often easily identifiable by the flange at the mouth to take the cover, or by an unglazed or ungilt rim, or simply as a question of proportion. Occasionally, on later Worcester or Derby, the mouth is gilt under the cover and one can be misled (p.479).

Watch for replaced covers that do not quite fit. Check damage on handles, mouth, base, cover and knop — the most vulnerable points. Note also that a vase has been seen with the handles broken off, the area where they were, ground down and then resprayed and gilded.

Worcester vases at the junction of socle and body were, between 1890 and 1920, very poorly joined with slip before firing. They break cleanly at this point and any restoration is difficult to detect.

Signed paintings on vases are generally of greater interest than those unsigned and many artists are recorded with their dates in the standard reference books. We have never yet seen a famous signature, such as Davis or Stinton, added to an anonymous vase, but no doubt that will come.

Vases

Belleek third quarter of the 19th century
Height 16ins:40.6cm. Black printed crest

A rare and desirable piece of Belleek, both for its large size and good
coloration; it is also well moulded. An uncoloured example £60–£80
and a late piece with the added County Fermanagh, Ireland to the crest
£30–£50.

£120–£150

Brownfield and Son c.1875
Height 9¼ins:23.5cm. Printed globes mark

A parian vase in the same matt coloration as the following piece, the body apricot and the leaves putty-coloured with white flowers. Pair £200–£240.

£80–£120

Vases

Brownfield and Son c.1875
Height 10 ⅞ ins: 27.5cm. Printed and impressed names

A stylish and well executed parian vase with pierced outer body gilt with Celtic motifs on the coral-scaled ground. Found in other colours. Pair £200–£250.

£80–£120

Brown-Westhead, Moore and Co. c.1870
Height 15¾ins:40cm. No mark

A high quality piece from a factory little known for this type of ware, the white figure seated on gilt and apricot sheaths forming vases. Pair £120–£150.

£50–£70

Vases

Brown-Westhead, Moore & Co. c.1870
Height 23ins:58.5cm. No mark

A fine pair of vases with well painted classical scenes on an apple-green
ground with flowers at the base and gilt handles. An uncommon factory
for large pieces of this sort. Pair £500—£700.

£200—£250

Coalport first quarter of the 19th century
Height 4¾ins:12cm. No mark

An attractive flower-painted vase in bright enamels, reserved on a pink ground with gilt borders. It is worth comparing this vase with the Rockingham vase on p.421 which, although a little larger, is as well painted but without the coloured ground.

£30–£40

Vases

Coalport c.1840
Height 12ins:30cm. Painted name

A sad example of the dying of a good vase. One handle has completely vanished, the other almost, and most of the flowers have been plucked. However the painting is good and the main body of the vase undamaged. With handles ground off, the flowers repaired where possible, or again ground off and restored, it will probably appear on the market at about £50–£60.

£30–£40

Coalport 1861
Height 25¼ins:64cm. Gilt ampersand

A very good vase in a sorry state with several severe body cracks. An important vase, as it was shown at the 1862 Exhibition and was illustrated in Waring's *Masterpieces of the 1862 Exhibition*. It was probably painted by R.F. Abrahams. A comparable perfect example £1,000–£1,500.

£520 (damaged)

Vases

Coalport c.1861
Height 15½ins:39.4cm. CBD monogram

A superb pair of rose-pompadour ground vases with brilliantly painted scenes after Boucher. The rope handles and other details picked out in gilding. The factory had a reputation at the time for the success of its pink ground but the production of the body suffered at the junction with the foot, where it is likely to become detached. Such damage does not greatly affect the price. The CBD monogram stands for Coalbrookdale.

£1,500–£1,800

Coalport c.1861
Height 30¼ins:76.8cm. Gilt ampersand

A large and very high quality vase and cover, probably made for the 1862 Exhibition. The putti in clouds were probably painted by James Rouse who later became the star decorator at Derby. The bleu-céleste ground is gilt with scroll work. It is highly unlikely that this vase ever had a companion, but a similar pair could be £4,000–£8,000.

£2,000–£3,000

Vases

Coalport 1897
Height 21¼ins:54cm. Printed name, retailer's name, limitation

A large and well executed vase made to commemorate the 1897 Diamond Jubilee. The small medallions on one side show scenes of the time when the Queen came to the throne in 1837, and on the other the same updated, i.e. reaping by hand and then mechanically. Only 50 were made for Osler's of Oxford St. One of the few exceptions to the rule that coronation or commemorative wares are of little value.

£800–£1,000

Coalport 1898
Height 7ins:17.8cm. Printed name, registration

A small pair of vases with deep blue body painted with scenes within lemon-yellow panels. Rather too 'dumpy' both in form and decoration to be generally desirable but in this case their small size brings them into the miniature category, of which there are many collectors.

£100–£150

Vases

Coalport c.1900
Height 7ins:18cm. Printed name

A three-handled vase with good gilding on the dark-blue ground enclosing small landscapes. This example was sold with one damaged handle for £42, which gives an idea of how very little damage can dramatically reduce values.

£100–£150

Coalport c.1900
Height 12ins:30.5cm. Printed name

A vase painted with fruit and leaves in a gilt-edged panel on a blue ground. A popular type of vase which can fetch more than it possibly deserves. A pair £700–£900.

£350–£400

Coalport c.1920
Height 10¼ins:26.1cm. Printed name, retailer's mark

A good pair of vases and covers with well painted fruit panels by F.H. Chivers, signed, on a royal-blue ground. Fine quality Coalport has been rising quite fast recently to bring it more in line with the Royal Worcesters and Derbys. A single vase and cover £250–£350.

£800–£1,000

Copeland c.1860
Height 11ins:28.5cm. No mark

A crisp and clean pair of parian vases doubled-walled and pierced and moulded with the female masks of the sun and moon within green and gilding. High quality pieces of this sort are still underpriced.

£80–£120

Vases

Copeland 1862
Height 17¼ins:44cm. Printed name

A fine vase, one of a pair £500—£800, painted by C.F. Hürten and exhibited at the 1862 Exhibition. The neck and foot with blue leaves and gilding on a pink ground, and all of a high standard. The knop in ormolu.

£200–£250

Copeland 1870
Height 15ins:38.1cm. Printed, WTC monogram and dated

A damaged piece brilliantly painted by C.F. Hürten, signed. It was executed for, and exhibited at, the 1871 Exhibition and is illustrated in the catalogue. The initials are those of W.T. Copeland, the owner of the factory. A comparable perfect piece £500–£800. C.F. Hürten was one of the best flower painters of the period, his work appearing at the major exhibitions. A very large vase, possibly his masterpiece, is in the Victoria & Albert Museum.

£180–£220 (damaged)

Vases

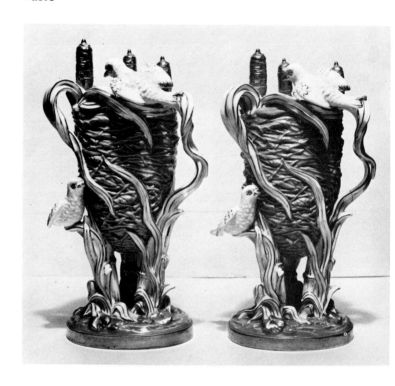

Copeland 1874
Height 9¾ins:25cm. Impressed name and date code

An amusing and well executed pair of vases, the nest turquoise and the rest with gilt lining. Cheap.

£40–£60

Copeland 1891–1902
Height 10¼ins:26cm. Printed name

The shoulders in apple-green and gilding above clear and naturalistic flowers, painting by F. Adams, signed. Copeland vases of this quality and date are not common and are sought after. As always, single vases are much less expensive.

£300–£400

Vases

Copeland c.1900
Height 16¼ins:41.5cm. Printed name

A richly-decorated pair of vases with 18th century figure subjects by S. Alcock, signed, the rest of the body deep-blue and gilt scrolled. Alcock was amongst the better late 19th century painters and the large size of these makes them highly desirable. A damaged knop would reduce the price by about £40.

£500–£800

Copeland and Garrett 1833—47
Height 5ins:12.6cm. Printed wreath

A dainty pair of spill vases with attractive painting and gilding. Less fussy than the flower-encrusted type and now more popular. Single £25—£30.

£75—£100

Vases

Davenport 1815-25
Height 10½ins:27cm. Davenport Longport

Porcelain vase in the Paris Empire style. Decorated with raised and tooled gilt agricultural trophies on a matt blue ground. Handles in the form of female heads. Vases and ornamental wares from this factory from before 1840 are very rare. Pair £250–£350.

Single vase: £90–£140

Derby Crown Porcelain Company 1885
Height 18½ins:47cm. Printed crowned monogram and date code

A superb quality vase, designed by H. Warrington Hogg, but lacking its cover, with very pale gold gilding on a cream ground with metallic red and green flowers and with matt and burnished gilt borders. **Pair £700–£900. Pair with cover £1,200–£1,500.**

£250–£350

Royal Crown Derby 1889
Height 5¾ins:14.6cm. Printed crowned monogram and date code

A washed-out yellow ground combined with appallingly insensitive gilding makes these amongst the least desirable wares from a much collected factory with a usually high standard. There was a period in the 1880s when a lot of bad gilding was done, see also p.377.

£80–£150

Royal Crown Derby 1891
Height 8¼ins:20.7cm. Printed crowned monogram and date code

A pair of eccentrically designed vases with gilt handles and decoration on a rose-pompadour ground. The painting is unfortunately not of the best, with a resulting lowish price. Even slightly better decoration £150–£200. Very thinly cast and therefore prone to damage, single £40–£50.

£120–£150

Vases

Royal Crown Derby 1892

Height 12½ins:31.9cm. Printed crowned monogram and date code

A popular type of decoration with iron-red, underglaze-blue and gilt flowers, some outlined in relief gilding, but with an overall somewhat confused appearance. Pair £400–£500.

£150–£200

Royal Crown Derby 1893
Height 11¾ins:30cm. Printed crowned monogram and date code

A maroon ground vase with gilt hog-weed, overall a dull appearance.
Pair £200–£300.

£80–£100

Royal Crown Derby 1904
Height 16¾ins:42.6cm. Printed crowned monogram, date code

An exceptionally large vase painted by W. Mosley, signed, with flowers on a gros-bleu ground, gilt with scrolls. The large size and high standard makes this a particularly desirable piece of Derby. The mark also has the Royal Coat of Arms.

£1,200–£1,500

Royal Crown Derby 1910
Height 14ins:35.5cm. Printed crowned monogram, date code

The flower painting by S. Hardy, signed and with good gilding on the gros-bleu ground. As always with Royal Crown Derby of this date a highly proficient production.

£200–£250

Vases

Royal Crown Derby 1911
Height 5¾ins:14.7cm. Printed crowned monogram, date code

A small vase with the 1128 Imari pattern. The same size and shape with a less popular design would be as little as £15–£20. Pair as illustrated £100–£150.

£40–£60

Doulton Late 19th century
Height 11¾ins:30cm. Printed rosette

The roses against a deep-blue ground and with gilt leaves. Because Doulton produced so much interesting stoneware in the late 19th century its porcelain, which was never very exciting, is largely unappreciated. The factory did not receive its 'Royal' title until 1901.

£140–£160

Grainger, Lee & Co. c.1830
Height, largest 11ins:28cm. Painted name

A garniture of vases with panels of flowers on a gros-bleu ground above gilt springing leaves. An uncommon set. Pair £350–£400, single large £150–£200.

£600–£800

Grainger and Co. 1850-70
Height 5½ins:14cm. Printed name

Well pierced and gilt bodies painted with small panels of flowers, originally had covers.

£200–£300.

Vases

Grainger and Co. 1870-89
Height $7\frac{1}{8}$ ins: 18cm. Printed shield

A well pierced vase and cover with simple gilt line details. The more elaborate the design of the piercing the more expensive the piece will be. A net has been defined as a lot of holes held together by string and it appears that the more these wares resemble holes held together by porcelain the more they are appreciated.

£250–£350

Grainger and Co. 1870-89
Height 10ins:25.4cm. Printed shield

A pair of vases with a creamy matt ground with gilt-edged leaves and pink flowers. Rather too plain to attract a very high price, they also had covers originally. With covers £150–£180.

£100–£150

Vases

Grainger and Co. c.1875
Height 9½ins: 24cm. Printed shield

A moon flask decorated with printed outlines of coloured sprigs and a butterfly against a duck-egg blue ground. The sparse decoration relieved a little by the gilt mask and snake handles. Pair £80–£100.

£30–£40

Grainger and Co. c.1880
Height 9½ins:24cm. Moulded KL monogram

A well-decorated pâte-sur-pâte vase, probably by one of the large family of Lockes whose initials appear on the base. Contemporary photographs show this shape as Grainger's, where the father, Edward, worked for a time before he set up the short-lived Locke's Worcester factory producing Royal Worcester style vases. Despite the high quality of the decorations, as with many other pâte-sur-pâte artists, apart from Solon, the work is underrated.

£100–£150.

Vases

Grainger and Co. 1890
Height 7¾ins: 19.8cm. Printed shield and registration

An amusingly conceived pair of vases with a little gilding and pierced bodies and necks. Grainger's pierced work was of as high a standard as that of Royal Worcester, excluding the individual work of George Owen and the paste used is an attractive, slightly matt, ivory tint, more sympathetic than the Royal factory's counterpart.

£150–£220

Grainger and Co. c.1890
Height 8¼ins: 21cm. Printed shield

An attractive vase with pierced and gilt spirals. With all pierced wares of
this type it is worth examining the piece with great care as it is possible
to damage one small scroll leaving an almost unnoticeable hole or hair
crack. Pair of these £220–£320.

£100–£120

Vases

Grainger & Co. 1891
Height 7½ins: 19cm. Printed shield and date code

The deep blue body with gilt and grey-blue hops. The neck very badly pierced. Pair £80–£120.

£20–£40

Grainger and Co. 1891-1900
Height 12ins:30.5cm. Printed shield

An extraordinarily designed pair of vases with the form based on the Chinese *ku* of a Shang dynasty bronze and the pierced scrolling both Indian and Moorish influenced. The result is not altogether comfortable especially as the casting is rather heavily executed and unrelieved by gilding. Examples may be found decorated with gilding £180–£220.

£150–£180

Vases

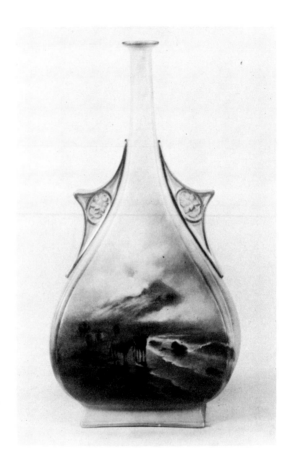

Grainger and Co. 1900
Height 9¼ins:23.5cm. Printed shield and date code

A little more unusual in form than most Grainger's and with an obviously J. Stinton-influenced design of Highland cattle on a peachy-yellowy ground, but unsigned.

£80–£120

J. Hadley & Sons 1900
Height 11ins:28cm. Printed name, date

A tyg with coloured slip decoration and painted orchids, gilt details.
Like most of Hadley's products, of good quality and unusual coloration.

£50–£70

Vases

George Jones 1874-91
Height 6ins:15.3cm. Impressed initials

A pâte-sur-pâte vase decorated by F. Schenk, signed, against a deep
green body, the ring handles gilt. Schenk was a competent artist in the
medium but his work has not been much collected, possibly partly due
to the dumpy shape supplied by George Jones and the uninteresting
gilding. Prices have risen sharply over the last year.

£150–£180

Minton c.1840
Height 28ins:71cm. No mark

A porcellanous tour-de-force, but despite the brilliance of the painting of the figure scenes and the richness and high standard of the flower-encrustation, the price is affected by as mundane a reason as the difficulty of cleaning it without pieces breaking off. Because of this such vases are rarely found perfect; it is indeed unlikely that they ever left the factory without some restoration and a certain amount is therefore acceptable. As it is almost impossible to display safely unless under a glass dome, the price is again affected adversely. Despite the lack of mark the shape is known and illustrated as the 'Very large Dresden vase' number 230 in the 1840 Minton design book. It is interesting that the cost of the vase included £3.12s.0d. for the figure painting and 5/- for the floral bouquet on the cover.

£800–£1,200

Vases

Minton c.1845
Height 10½ins.:26.8cm. No mark

A fine vase after a Sèvres original, well painted with exotic birds and with blue, pink and gilt borders and handles. The type is known as Sneyn from the design record books and was on view at the 1849 Birmingham Exhibition. Pair £400–£600.

£120–£180

Minton 1862
Height 4¾ins:12cm. Painted name and impressed date code

With better moulding these could have been quite attractive vases, the body pale and the leaves dark green and with white lily of the valley flowers. This pair are in reasonable condition, most of the flowers intact. Any damage would reduce the price to £8—£10.

£30—£50

Vases

Minton 1862
Height 16ins:41.7cm. Printed ermine mark

Well painted in bright enamels, the blue-céleste ground with fine tooled gilding. The dancing maidens not a highly desirable subject. Single £200–£300. These vases were shown at the 1862 Exhibition in London and bear the puce ermine mark used only on those pieces.

£500–£800

Mintons 1867
Height 11½ins:29cm. Impressed name and registration

An unusual design of matt and burnished acid-etched gilt borders and ovals against a mirror-black ground. A well-finished vase but not very desirable because of the colour, pair £80–£120. If found in another colour, they would be £120+.

£25–£35

Vases

Minton 1870
Height 10½ins:26.6cm. Impressed name with date code

The Aesthetic or Japanese Movement is now gathering its second impetus and prices have started to rise. Vases such as these which, apart from period interest are also decorative, sell as such. The bright turquoise ground with motifs on the feet and shoulders based on oriental cloisonné.

£250–£300

Minton 1871
Height 20ins:50.8cm. Impressed name and date code

A good pair of vases with brightly enamelled birds. The blue ground is rather too dark resulting in an unfortunate drab appearance; a brighter blue or other colour could raise the price to £600 or £800. The handles and borders gilt. Single vase £150—£180.

£500—£550

Vases

Minton 1871
Height 14½ins:37cm. Impressed name and date code

An important clock garniture in pâte-sur-pâte by M.L. Solon. Solon
came to England from Sèvres in 1870 and had this garniture ready for
the 1871 London International Exhibition where it was shown on the
stand of Thomas Goode. It was also illustrated in the Art Journal
Catalogue. It is difficult to assess accurately pieces as important as this
set, which had some damage to covers and opened firing faults, the
price being dependent on so many factors.

£1,500–£2,500

Minton probably 1871
Height 10ins:25.4cm. Impressed name and blurred date code

One of the oriental-influenced wares of the 1870's and 80's which are underpriced. Well decorated and gilt but not popular. A pair would be much better at £140–£180, but still the price compares unfavourably with, for example, a pair of Royal Worcester vases with sheep. This shape with the small loop handles has been seen with the handles broken off, ground down and restored.

£60–£80

Vases

Mintons 1874
Height 12ins:30.5cm. Impressed name and date code

A pale pink soft porcelain body with gilt-printed roundles. A plain but interesting moon flask from a design point of view. The fish are taken from the Chinese fish moulded in low relief on marriage ceremony dishes and the stylisation of the butterfly could suggest a 1920s date. The type of item that is unappreciated by all but a few enthusiasts for the history of ceramic design. Pair £30—£60.

£10—£20

Mintons possibly 1875
Height 7 $\frac{7}{8}$ ins: 17.1cm.
Printed name and retailer's mark, blurred date code

This set of vases is very thinly potted and intricately pierced and therefore fragile. Few examples seem to have survived. The rose-pompadour ground has gilt-edged panels of putti resting on clouds. All of good quality and desirable.

£450–£500

Vases

Minton c.1880
Height 6½ins:16.5cm. Printed impressed names

A dull pair of vases, the shoulders in simulated bronze and with silvered and gilt flowers on a pale lilac ground. The idea of the bronze bands is taken from Chinese porcelain of the same date where it is equally dreary.

£20–£25

Mintons 1887
Height 15½ins:39.5cm.
Printed gilt crowned globe and impressed date code

A superb, coloured, pâte-sur-pâte vase by M.L. Solon, signed, with an elaborate design of putti being weighed. The borders in green, yellow, brown and gilding. The technique of pâte-sur-pâte was extremely slow and fraught with dangers of failure and, therefore, very expensive at the time. This particular vase is highly successful and the subject matter is easier to take than many of Solon's designs. Pair £4,000–£6,000.

£1,200–£1,800

Vases

Mintons 1888
Height 11½ins:29.2cm.
Gilt and impressed crowned globe and name, date code

A superb piece of pâte-sur-pâte but unsigned, possibly by A. Birks. The body a deep blue-green and the interior is also decorated in gilt with a flaming sun motif.

£500–£600

Mintons c.1890
Height 6ins:15cm. No mark

The pâte-sur-pâte panel by T. Mellor, signed and inscribed 'after A. Boullemier'. The body in page pink-red with blue ribbons, the white figures against midnight-blue. T. Mellor was one of Solon's pupils and his work is rare; it is additionally unusual to have recorded the name of the artist after whom the design is taken. Pair £200–£250.

£60–£120

Vases

Mintons c.1890
Height 15¾ins:38.7cm.
Printed crown and globe, impressed name and retailer's name

A pâte-sur-pâte vase of fine quality but unfortunately unsigned. The body a deep sea-green and a very common shape for pâte-sur-pâte decoration. M.L. Solon who trained several apprentices to help in the work, was said to disapprove of anyone but himself signing their work, although after 1900 this became more common. The mark of the retailer is often found on pieces such as this, in this case Thomas Goode.

£400–£600

Minton 1894

Height 8¾ins:22.2cm. Impressed name and date code

A rare M.L. Solon vase with a white figure in pâte-sur-pâte against the 'artificial ruby' ground which changes colour according to the light in which it is viewed. The combination of bichrome of potash and alumina changes from mushroom in daylight to deep-carmine in tungsten.

£400–£600

Mintons c.1895
Height 21½ins:54cm. Blurred impressed marks

One of an unusual pair of vases in that there are seven different colours of pâte-sur-pâte involved. The panels are by H. Hollins, signed, and the whole design is not particularly successful. The body is also too big for the foot. Hollins was one of Solon's apprentices but by no means one of the best. Compare with the Solon vase (page 409).

£1,500–£1,800 (pair)

Mintons 1895-1900
Height 8½ins:21.6cm. Printed gilt crowned globe, date code

A deep aquamarine body with white figures by M.L. Solon, signed. Typical subject and the usual good gilt borders. The standard of the pâte-sur-pâte is unusually crisp and clear and the price reflects this. The date codes on pâte-sur-pâte of this date are frequently blurred and difficult to decipher but one can usually make out enough of an outline to give bracket figures.

£600–£800

Vases

Mintons 1902
Height 9ins:23cm. Printed crowned globe, impressed date code

A pâte-sur-pâte vase by Alboine Birks with his monogram. The argument over whether Solon or his pupil Birks was the better pâte-sur-pâte artist ultimately rests on one's own taste but certainly Birks's handling of naturalistic foliage and flowers was streaks ahead of his master's, while his putti appear to have taken weight-lifting courses.

£500–£600

Moore 1873
Height 8ins:20.3cm. Impressed registration

A good quality vase in the form of a putto supporting a fan, hollow to form a vase. Like the Brown-Westhead, Moore example not a much collected style especially as the bird painting on the fan is beginning to reflect the Japanese taste with a resultant clash of cultures. Pair £100–£120.

£40–£60

Vases

Moore 1875
Height 6¾ins:17.2cm. Impressed name

The knop is missing from the top of this 'Vaisseau à Mât' (literally boat with mast). A perfect example £60–£80. Copied from 18th century Sèvres originals.

£30–£50 (damaged)

Moore c.1895
Height 4ins:10.2cm. Impressed name

A pair of vases in the form of epiphyllum cacti, a favourite form, not only of Moore's, but of several other factories of the last quarter of the 19th century. The flowers pale yellow and with base gilt on the poorly-moulded ground. These can be found in several sizes; 6in., £60–£80; 8ins., £150.

£40–£60

Vases

Rockingham 1826-42
Height 4ins:10cm. Printed griffin in puce

A small and not very attractive piece of porcelain painted with uninspired flowers on a blue ground. Without the factory mark this vase would fetch about £15–£20. Although the shape is unique to the factory, an unmarked piece would fetch £15–£20. A really well painted piece £150–£200.

£80–£120

Rockingham 1826-42
Height 5¾ins:14.5cm. Printed griffin in puce

An attractively painted vase with typical early nineteenth century flowers including the popular ranunculus and passion flower reserved in a gilt panel on a green ground. The shape is common to many factories and a mark is vital for identification, but look out for added marks. Prices vary according to period and the decoration.

£60–£150

Rockingham 1830-42
Height 10¾ins:27.2cm. Printed griffin in puce

One of the few vases of a type at one time always called Rockingham which actually is. The scene of a ruined abbey is rather mean in size but the bizarre stork-head handles help a great deal. The applied flowers not of the best. Made in other sizes: 6¼in:16cm. £120–£150.

£200–£220

Spode first quarter of the 19th century
Height 4½ins:11.5cm. Painted name

A typical Imari pattern of the period with the usual stylised flowers and fenced garden. Because they are not uncommon and not large enough to score on their decoration alone, vases such as these are not expensive. Single £20–£30.

£60–£80

Vases

Spode c.1820-30
Height 10¼ins:26cm. Painted name

A fine pair of vases in neo-classical style and well painted with named scenes of mythological subjects. The handles gilt and all of high quality. Well painted figure subjects of this type are very saleable and considerably rarer than simple floral studies.

£800–£1,000

Spode 1965
Height 13½ins:34.2cm. Gilt printed marks including name

A limited edition covered vase of reasonable quality with a wealth of detail about Sir Winston Churchill's life and honours. Like most commemorative wares liable to violent ups and downs in price but, being one of only 125, probably with a good chance of survival.

£100–£150

Vases

Swansea 1819
Height 4½ins:11.5cm. Painted name

A rare pair of spill vases entertainingly painted with oriental influenced deer in panels reserved on a flower-painted ground. These vases are of additional interest in that they bear the initials MM, probably those of the painter Mary Moggridge, and the date 1819. Without initials and date £300–£400.

£500–£700

Wedgwood 1920's
Height 8¼ins:21cm. Printed vase and name

A pair of mottled pale blue-ground vases with gilt and mottled purple dragons above waves. Not being decorated with fairies, they are relatively inexpensive.

£140–£180

Vases

Wedgwood 1920's
Height 7¼ins:18.5cm. Printed vase and name

A pair of vases with plum and gilt dragons against a pale runny blue ground. The pale ground make the dragons better delineated than usual with a higher price. Pairs of these are much less common than singles but, in contradiction to normal practice, little more expensive.

£180–£220

Wedgwood 1920's
Height 9½ins:24.2cm. Printed vase and name

This print of a fairy is not common and when seen is rarely well coloured and registered. As can be seen her dress is blurred and the whole rather too dark. A good clear design could fetch £300–£350.

£200–£300

Vases

Wedgwood 1920's
Height 11¼ins:28.5cm. Printed vase and name

A fine vase with good registration of the gilding over bright colours.
Pair £1,200–£1,400.

£450–£500

Wedgwood 1920's
Height 16½ins:41.9cm. Printed vase and name

An exceptionally large piece of Fairyland and with very bright coloration. This particular shape is rare.

£800–£1,000

Vases

Wedgwood 1920's
Height 11½ins:29cm. Printed vase and name

A well-matched pair of fairyland vases with a complicated but accurately registered design of a snake round a tree and dreamlike happenings in bright enamels and gilding.

£1,000–£1,500

Wedgwood c.1930
Height 11ins:28cm. Printed vase and name

Coloured butterflies against mottled blue ground. As with the dragons lustre not expensive compared with the Fairyland. Given the same size, any other form of vase with the same design would be about the same price.

£150–£200

Vases

Worcester, Flight, Barr and Barr c.1820
Height 12ins:30.5cm. Printed name

A fine covered vase painted with shells on one side and flowers on the other, probably by Thomas Baxter. The ground deep blue with gilt scrolls and handles.

£1,000–£1,200

Worcester, Flight, Barr and Barr c.1820
Height 6½ins:16.5cm. Printed name

A blue ground vase with a panel of Faith and with gilt details. The religious subject is against the piece making as much as a landscape £400–£600. Pair of Faith and Hope £900–£1,400. Pair with landscapes £1,000–£1,500.

£350–£500

Vases

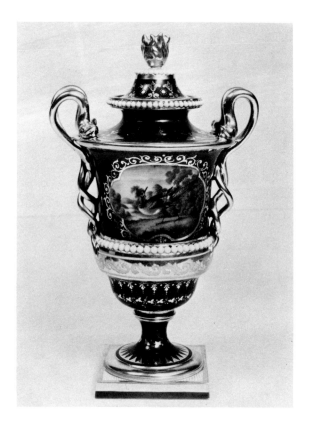

Worcester, Flight, Barr and Barr c.1820
Height 8½ins:21.5cm. Painted name

A vase and cover with gilt snake handles and a blue ground painted with a panel of an exotic bird in a landscape by 'Dr.' George Davis. Pair £1,000–£1,500. Single with damaged handles £250–£300. A clean break at the junction of socle and body is not uncommon and does not affect the price by more than about 10%.

£400–£500

Worcester, Flight, Barr and Barr c.1820
Height 7ins:17.8cm. Printed name

An urn with deep blue ground painted with a panel of flowers, pair
£600–£800.

£250–£350

Vases

Worcester, Flight, Barr and Barr c.1830
Height 8ins:20.3cm. Printed name

A vase and cover with a panel of Clio within a beaded border on a green ground supported on the heads of three gilt mermen, one of whom lacks wings. Perfect example £450–£550. Without matching cover £150–£200.

£350–£450 as illustrated

Worcester, Kerr and Binns 1858
Height 8¾ins:21.3cm. Printed shield and date

A high quality pair of vases painted in grey with titled portraits of classical authors, the rest with tooled gilding. Kerr and Binns period Worcester is underpriced at the moment, probably because there is too little of it about to generate a strong market.

£70–£90

Vases

Worcester, Kerr and Binns c.1860
Height approx. 4ins:10cm. Printed shield

A pair of spill vases with classical heads in grey, the ground bleu-de-roi
and gilt with wreaths. Wares from this period are not common and tend
to be underpriced.

£80–£120

Royal Worcester 1862
Height 7ins:17.8cm. Printed crowned circle and date code

A pair of vases and covers painted in white enamel by Thomas Bott on
a turquoise ground. Lacking covers £180–£250.

£350–£400

Vases

Royal Worcester 1863
Height 6ins:15cm. Printed crowned circle, date code

A rare parian piece with unusual pink, purple, brown and green coloration picked out in gilding. Good quality but not the most attractive of objects. Nor of a much collected period. A pair would be more desirable to the decorators £80–£120.

£30–£40

Royal Worcester 1866
Height 12ins:30.5cm. Printed name

A fine vase with a deep blue ground enamelled in white by Thomas Bott with putti in 'Limoges Style'. Such pieces are rare and much sought after, his work being exhibited from 1851 to 1870 when he died. Not to be confused with his son, T.J. Bott, who also worked at Worcester c.1870-1885 in the same style as his father.

£600–£900

Vases

Royal Worcester 1867 and c.1870
Height 6¾ins:17.2cm.
Impressed and printed crowned circle, one with date code

A comparison showing the same shape treated in different ways. The example on the left with coloured flowers, gilt borders, turquoise medallions and white beads £30–£50, the other with pale apricot ground and gilt borders, much less desirable £15–£20. It is worth comparing also the sharpness of the moulding on the example on the left with the other.

Royal Worcester 1872
Height 8¼ins: 21cm. Printed crowned circle mark and dated 1872

A good pair of Japanese-taste vases after James Hadley with the portraits tinted against a bronzed ground by James Callowhill, the handles and feet also with bronzing and gilding. These and other vases in similar style were exhibited at the London International Exhibition of 1871-72 and were illustrated in the Art Journal Catalogue. The standard of production is very high and this, combined with their period interest, would seem to indicate a likely rapid increase in price.

£400–£500

Vases

Royal Worcester 1874
Height 10¼ins:26.7cm. Impressed and printed crowned circle, date code

One of Hadley's Japanese series with ivory-tinted body and sombre but
very well executed coloration. Should be a pair £400–£600.

£180–£220

Royal Worcester last quarter of the 19th century
Height 9ins:22.8cm. Printed crowned circle, registration

A model after James Hadley. The animal with brown howdah and brightly enamelled details picked out in gilding. A popular, uncommon and amusing beast also found in a number of other colour schemes, e.g. white £50–£80; white and celadon £70–£100; peach, yellow and gilt £200–£300.

£400–£600

Vases

Royal Worcester c.1875
Height 10ins:25.4cm. Impressed crowned circle, registration mark

After a model by James Hadley, with his moulded signature, sage green body with gilt details, the howdah on the back forming a vase. A rarer piece than the elephant. Coloured example £130—£200.

£100—£150

Royal Worcester 1876

Height 3¼ins:8.5cm. Printed crowned circle and dated

A most entertaining little vase in Japanese taste, the frog bronzed and gilt on a yellow ground. Quite uncommon and underpriced.

£25–£30

Vases

Royal Worcester 1879
Height 7⅞ ins : 20cm. Printed crowned circle, date code

An amusing vase with the owl in two tones of gold and of good quality.

£100–£120

Royal Worcester 1879
Height 11½ins:29.3cm.
Printed crowned circle, date code and
retailer's mark Tiffany and Co, New York

A good moon flask with matt-coloured and gilt flowers, the moulded handle and base in silver and gilding. The addition of the retailer's mark makes the vase more interesting but does not affect the value. Pair £300–£400.

£100–£150

Vases

Royal Worcester 1880
Height $3\frac{1}{8}$ ins: 8cm. Printed crowned circle, date code

A multiple vase after an oriental original with a crudely-coloured spray of prunus attaching interlocking sections of bamboo. An amusing idea ruined by poor casting.

£10–£15

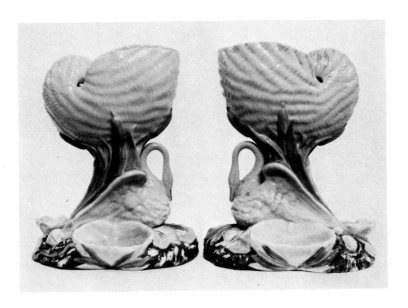

Royal Worcester 1880
Height 8ins:20.3cm. Impressed crowned circle mark, date code

A pair of shell vases weakly coloured in pink and green and reminiscent of Belleek. Not very sharply cast, but not a common form either.

£60–£70

Vases

Royal Worcester 1880
Height 11ins:28cm. Printed crowned circle, registration, date code

The flower-head background on this pair of vases is transfer-printed in grey and over painted with brightly enamelled and gilt butterflies and plants. The result is attractive and unusual. Outside the field of most Worcester collectors and therefore underpriced.

£60–£100

Royal Worcester 1880
Height 15½ins:39.5cm. Printed crowned circle and date code

A large and rare pair of Japanese taste vases modelled by James Hadley, whose moulded signature appears on one. The figures are in relief and coloured, apparently carved from a section of bamboo.

£800–£1,200

Vases

Royal Worcester 1881
Height 11ins:27.9cm. Impressed and printed crowned circle, date code

A shell wall pocket with a gilt coral branch. A difficult object to display in a cabinet and, as most collectors are not prepared to fix them to a wall as intended, they are relatively cheap. Pair £35–£45.

£15–£20

Royal Worcester 1882
Height 8ins:20.3cm. Printed crowned circle, date code

An attractive moon flask with bright yellow body well coloured with a mauve clematis and printed gilding. As always for this date and style, too cheap. Pair £70–£100.

£20–£30

Vases

Royal Worcester 1883
Height 14ins:36cm. Impressed and printed crowned circle, date code

A rare vase with a streaky yellow, brown and green glaze after a Chinese 'Tang' original and encircled by a silvery dragon, in this example heavily restored. A perfect example £100–£150.

£30–£50 (damaged)

Royal Worcester 1884
Height 14½ins:37cm. Printed and impressed crowned circle, date code

A pair of vases and covers in Eastern taste, the flowers in tones of gilding on a matt ivory ground, the covers pierced. This type of vase is often found lacking the cover, which is not always obvious from an examination of the mouth. The only reliable way is to check the shape number on the bottom with the list of shapes in Sandon (see bibliography) to see if it was made with one. Some vases still appear in proportion without their covers and are readily saleable, this pair without £200–£250.

£350–£450

Vases

Royal Worcester 1888
Height 23½ins:59.7cm.
Printed and impressed crowned circle, date code

A brilliant and rare example of the best porcelain of the period. The original modelled by James Hadley with his moulded signature. Richly and finely gilt on an ivory-coloured body with enamelled peacocks in bright colours. The vase was made for R.W. Binns, the firm's Art Director, and bears his monogram on the base. Vases of this quality appear very infrequently on the market and are those mostly likely to show a steep rise in price.

£2,000–£3,000

Royal Worcester 1890
Height 7ins:17.8cm. Printed crowned circle, code for 1890

A pencil note on the base of this piece records that there are 2,034 perforations. All these would have been cut without Owen using any guide lines to help him. His patterns are fairly standard and even on unsigned pieces his hand is unmistakeable.

£400–£500

Vases

Royal Worcester 1896
Height 19ins:48cm. Printed crowned circle, date code

A large and decorative vase of good quality painted with shaggy-looking flowers against the usual yellow-orange ground. The scrolling on the shoulders in relief on sage-green. Pair £800–£1,000.

£300–£350

Royal Worcester 1897

Height 10ins:25.5cm. Printed crowned circle and date code

Peach, yellow and gilt coloured, the swan has a vase incorporated in its body between the wings. A variation of the model has a putto holding a rein on the tail, £120–£150.

£100–£200

Vases

Hadley, Worcester 1897-1900
Height 9¾ins:24.7cm. Printed mark

Typical of Hadley's Worcester with the use of coloured clay slips looking remarkably like polychrome bubble-gum or putty. His productions were generally of good quality and are best when they depend purely on their form and colour, like this example, without being overpainted with birds or flowers etc. It does not follow, however, that a painted comparable piece will be cheaper. This with flowers £120–£150.

£100–£120

Royal Worcester 1899
Height 8ins:20.3cm.
Printed crowned circle, registration and date code

A well painted pair of vases by C. Baldwyn, signed, with a greenfinch and a chaffinch on gorse and apple blossom, gilt details. A refreshing change from the usual swans by this artist and showing the skill of which he was capable.

£500–£700

Vases

Royal Worcester 1900 and 1907
Height 16½ins:42cm. Printed crowned circle

A price-comparison between two vases of the same shape and size. The left example painted with chrysanthemums, the moulding of pale tone with gilding £150–£180, pair £400–£500. The right hand piece with a Highland cattle scene by John Stinton, signed, the rest of the body gold-speckled greenish-bronze. A far richer looking production £600–£800. Pair £1,200–£1,500.

Royal Worcester 1900
Height 8ins:20.3cm. Printed crowned circle

This and the following vase are about as near as English porcelain ever got to the art nouveau movement, although it flowered profusely in pottery. In neither case would it be recognised by the Continental purist.

£30–£50

Vases

Royal Worcester 1901
Height 12ins:30.5cm. Printed crowned circle, date code

A slightly nearer attempt at art nouveau than the previous vase, the aquilegias in enamels with gilt outlines and with gilt tendril handles. Pair £120–£200.

£60–£100

Royal Worcester 1902

Height 5ins:13cm. Printed crowned circle, date code

A very simple, but typical, 'Japanese' design first produced in 1874, of which this is obviously a late example, a pair £20–£30.

£8–£12

Vases

Royal Worcester 1903
Height 3½ins:9cm. Printed crowned circle, date code

A small and poor Art Nouveau influenced vase made a little more interesting by the use of 'shot enamels' on the leaf feet. Without this coloration of greenish-reddish gilding, £8—£10.

£12—£18

Royal Worcester 1907
Height 8ins:20.3cm. Crowned circle, date code and Sabrina Ware

A Sabrina ware vase with a simple stencilled flower on a green and blue ground. Not one of the most satisfactory examples of a fairly uncommon type, better pieces up to £120, signed pieces are also more expensive.

£30–£50

Royal Worcester 1907
Height 9½ins:24.5cm.
Impressed and printed crowned circle, date code

A pair of Persian-influenced vases with pierced wing handles painted by C.H.C. Baldwyn, signed, with swans on a blue ground. See also the plate p.258.

£500–£600

Royal Worcester 1907
Height 21ins:53cm. Printed crowned circle, registration, date code

A superb pair of vases with apple green bodies and white relief scroll-work. The scenes after Boucher by William A. Hawkins, signed, and titled on the base Summer and Autumn. To fault these vases: the contrast of the dark green is too great with the white scrolls and the gilt beading round the panels is uninspired and serves only to cheapen the appearance. Small points, not enough to keep the vases out of the very top price bracket.

£2,000–£3,000

473

Vases

Royal Worcester 1908
Height 11¼ins:28.5cm. Printed crowned circle with date code

Signed vases by the Stintons, like these, have been rising rapidly in price over the last year. Large pairs with their covers are now very expensive, although this pair have by no means the best standard of gilding and colouring that the factory was capable of. Lacking covers £400–£600.

£700–£1,000

Royal Worcester 1909
Height 5⅛ ins: 13cm. Printed crowned circle, date code

Painted by E. Barker, signed, with a coal tit. A rather dull vase with an appropriately low price. Pair £70–£100.

£30–£40

Vases

Royal Worcester 1910
Height 8¾ins:22.2cm. Printed crowned circle, registration, date code

Each vase with large roses by H. Martin, signed, in pale yellow and pink,
the mouth, base and handles gilt.

£250–£280

Royal Worcester 1910
Height 10¾ins: 24.5cm. Printed crowned circle and date code

Painted with roses by H. Martin, signed, a somewhat mass-produced looking vase in green and red, gilt stem. Popular with collectors because of its size, an eight inch example only £50–£80.

£180–£220

Vases

Royal Worcester 1912
Height 7½ins:19cm. Printed crowned circle mark and date code

An uncommon type of vase of which several different patterns and shapes were produced up to the first world war. The designs are transfer-printed outlines of chinoiserie scenes brightly enamelled on top and often with a distinctive ground, this example with a grey simulated granite effect. The quality is always high and they never sell for very much.

£25–£35

Royal Worcester 1913
Height 7½ins:19cm. Printed crowned circle, date code

Rather a badly moulded vase painted with swans by C.H.C. Baldwyn, signed, against a sky-blue ground. As with most Royal Worcester pieces the mark includes the shape number, in this case 1937, which by reference to the list supplied in Henry Sandon's book tells us that the vase should have a cover. With the cover £150–£120.

£120–£150

Vases

Royal Worcester 1913
Height 8⅝ ins:22cm. Printed crowned circle, date code

The vase and cover pierced with angel heads and scrolls, the osprey in tones of peach and yellow and with gilt details. An uncommon and decorative piece obviously liable to damage on wing tips or cracked piercing, so watch for restoration.

£100–£130

Royal Worcester 1917
Height 5ins: 12.6cm. Printed crowned circle, date code

A quite well pierced vase in Grainger style. The pheasant painted by James Stinton, signed, pair £200–£250. Lacks cover.

£60–£80

Vases

Royal Worcester 1921
Height 8¾ins:22cm. Printed crowned circle, date code

Although uncommon, these vases painted by Ernest Barker, signed, are
inexpensive for several reasons: the scenes are too small, the pastel
tones of the gilt border are too weak and the gilding is rubbed. Barker's
sheep paintings were quite as good as those of Harry Davis, but
generally much less expensive. A perfect pair still only £60–£80.

£50–£70

Royal Worcester 1923
Height 8¼ins:21cm. Printed crowned circle, date code

Painted by Harry Davis, signed, with sheep in a landscape. The base moulded as a stand and gilt. Davis's sheep painting is a great deal more common than is his pure landscape and often less good. It is, however, more popular. All Worcester painters had their own particular forte and could produce this endlessly to order. When they stepped outside this niche, the piece was often more interesting but tends to be less expensive.

£350–£400

Vases

Royal Worcester 1926
Height 8ins:20.2cm. Printed crowned circle, date code

Despite the scarcity of Royal Worcester fairyland-influenced lustre wares they are not expensive or sought after. The colours are here a brilliant flame orange, green and gilding and technically as competent as the Wedgwood examples but lack the exciting designs.

£30–£40

Unattributed first quarter of the 19th century
Height 3½ins:9cm. No mark

A pair of dull and badly painted vases typical of much poor quality wares turned out in the doldrum period at the beginning of the century. The gilding is particularly uninspired and note how badly formed the beading is above the foot. Such wares are often haphazardly attributed to Derby on the strength of a similarity of paste and shape.

£20–£40

Vases

Probably Minton early 19th century
Height 4ins:10cm. No mark

A small and well painted spill vase with an unidentified scene between gilt lines. Typical of the type of vase that would be attributed for no good reason to Derby or Rockingham. Certainly a Derby example would be marked as such. Pair £100–£150.

£40–£50

Unattributed first quarter of the 19th century
Height 4ins:10cm. No mark

A spili vase with an amusing scene of a sultan and a courtesan. It is interesting to compare this piece with the preceding vase painted with a landscape, which obviously owes its inspiration to the late 18th century, while the Arabian Nights subject is very much 19th century. It seems likely that in time this piece will show the greatest growth potential.

£40–£60

Vases

Minton c.1840
Heights 9¾ and 10½ins:24.7 and 26.8cm. No mark

Design No. 164. A garniture of well and brightly painted vases on a cobalt-blue ground, peach and gilt handles. Like a great deal of the reasonable quality ware of the 1830-60 period, these are undervalued. The sale of a good collection by auction or a book on the factory that produced them would help to raise the price, probably quite considerably.

£120–£200

Fakes

The collector of nineteenth and twentieth century British porcelain is fortunate in that, due to lack of previous interest in the period, little has been copied and is now likely to be copied because of the prohibitive cost of producing an article of any great value. His counterpart collector in the pottery field is on much shakier ground.

The most modern object I have seen is a Carltonware lustre vase with the mark erased, probably by hydrofluoric acid, and a printed Wedgwood mark substituted (figure 1): a reasonably well-executed fake, but on an earthenware body, not likely to fool anyone with a knowledge of the Fairyland patterns. A bird group has been reported with fake Royal Worcester Dorothy Doughty Pedigree and it seems likely that the faker's attention will be directed to the relatively easy job of doctoring marks, as has happened with the pair of Paris hard-paste porcelain vases (figure 2) which show an interesting variation on a theme. One vase has had a crudely transferred crowned circle mark and its pair a genuine printed mark cut from an object and stuck on (figures 3, 4). Neither of these should fool anyone even half awake.

Royal Worcester seems at the moment to be suffering most at the hands of the mark surgeon. The Grainger and Co. Worcester ewer (figure 5) has lost its original mark by grinding on a wheel, the streaks of light in the photograph show the body through the glaze, and has received a pseudo-Royal Worcester mark in its place (figure 6), pseudo not only in the sense that it is not genuine but that it never existed. The faker has combined elements of Royal Worcester marks without achieving reality; figure 7 shows genuine marks of the period.

In the 1830s and 40s some of the major factories are known to have produced copies of Continental objects, usually Sèvres, for which they were criticised at the time, and are cursed now, since we are unable to attribute the copies with any certainty. They did, however, reproduce English porcelain from the early nineteenth century factories, such as Nantgarw. The plate (figure 8) with an impressed mark (figure 9), is probably by Coalport.

Fakes

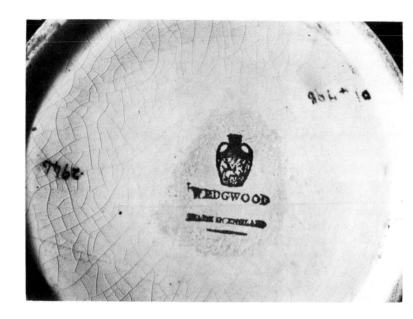

Figure 1

Figure 2

Fakes

Figure 3

Figure 4

Fakes

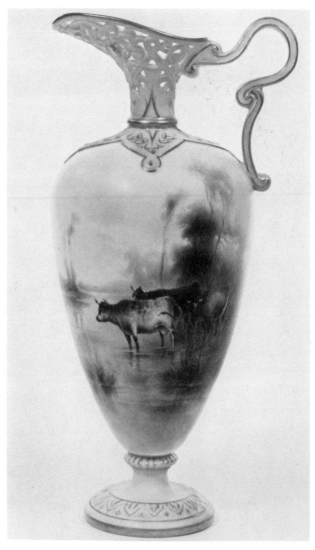

Figure 5

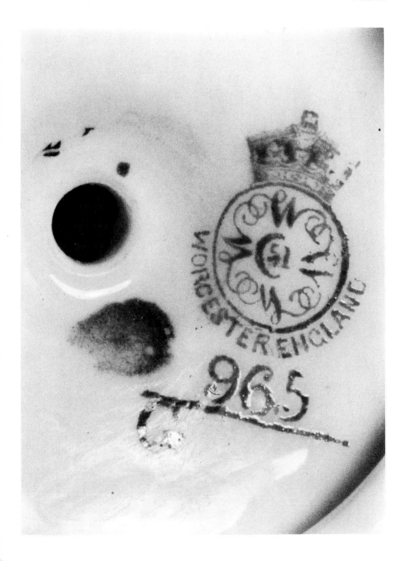

Figure 6

Figure 7

Figure 8

Fakes

Figure 9

Damage

The question of damage raises a number of problems and personal preferences. Some collectors, if they cannot find a perfect example, would rather have a damaged piece looking as near to its original condition as possible. To achieve this the modern restorer has developed an extraordinarily high standard of workmanship. Epoxy resin adhesives, kiln-hardened enamels and skilled painters can produce nearly undiscoverable repairs that do not yellow with age and are hard to the touch. They do, at the moment, show under ultra-violet light and feel dead when touched on the teeth – no doubt even this will change. When buying from a shop, it is vital to ask whether the piece is in any way restored and to insist on a receipt that states its date, factory and condition. A reliable shop will be only too happy to do this. Hesitation or refusal should put you on your guard.

The Worcester figure of a water carrier illustrates a method of cleaning up a cracked or chipped base with a technique more commonly associated with glass. The base has been ground smooth on a carborundum wheel until it appears perfect when viewed standing, although a little flat, but it exhibits a curious change of plane at one point on the underside, arrowed in the photograph (figures a and b).

Damage

Figure a.

Figure b.

Factories

1. **S. Alcock & Co.**, Cobridge, c.1828-53, Hill Pottery, Burslem, 1830-59.
2. **Belleek Pottery**, County Fermanagh, Ireland, 1863 to present day.
3. **John Bevington**, Kensington Works, Hanley, 1872-92.
4. **E.J.D. Bodley**, Hill Pottery, Burslem, 1875-92.
5. **W. Brownfield & Son**, Cobridge, 1850-91.
6. **Brown-Westhead, Moore & Co.**, Cauldon Place, Hanley, 1862-1904, later Cauldon.
7. **Cauldon**, Shelton, Hanley, 1905-20.
8. **E. & C. Challinor**, Fenton, 1862-91.
9. **R. Chamberlain**, Worcester, 1783-1840, later Chamberlain & Co.
10. **Chamberlain & Co.**, Worcester, 1840-1852.
11. **Coalport (Caughley)**, Coalport, Shropshire, 1795 to present day.
12. **W.T. Copeland & Sons**, Spode Works, Stoke, 1847 to present day.
13. **Copeland & Garrett**, Spode Works, Stoke, 1833-47, later W.T. Copeland.
14. **Davenport**, Longport, 1793-1887.
15. **Derby**, 1750-1848, 1878 to present day. Bloor Derby 1830-40, Derby Crown Porcelain Co. Ltd. 1876-90, Royal Crown Derby Porcelain Co. Ltd. 1890 to present day.
16. **Doulton & Co.**, Burslem, 1882 to present day. Royal Doulton from 1901.
17. **W.H. Goss, Goss and Peake**, Falcon Pottery, Stoke, 1858-1944.
18. **G. Grainger & Co.**, Worcester, 1839-1902.
19. **Grainger, Lee & Co.**, Worcester, 1812-1837, later G. Grainger & Co.
20. **J. Green**, retailer, London 1834-1874.
21. **J. Hadley & Sons**, High Street, Worcester, 1896-1905.

22. **Hill Pottery**, see S. Alcock.

23. **G. Jones,** various addresses in Stoke, 1864-1957.

24. **Kerr & Binns,** see Worcester.

25. **C. Meigh,** Old Hall Pottery, Hanley, 1835-61.

26. **Minton,** Stoke, 1793 to present day.

27. **Moore Brothers,** St. Mary's Works, Longton, 1872-1905.

28. **Nantgarw,** Glamorgan, Wales, c.1813-14 and 1817-22.

29. **New Hall Porcelain Works,** Shelton, Hanley, 1781-1835.

30. **Paragon,** Longton, 1920 to present day.

31. **Robinson and Leadbeater,** Stoke, 1864-1924.

32. **Rockingham Works,** Nr. Swinton, porcelain manufacture 1826-1842.

33. **J. Spode,** Stoke, c.1784-1833, later Copeland and Garrett.

34. **Swansea,** 1814-22.

35. **J. Wedgwood,** various addresses, 1759 to present day.

36. **Worcester,** Dr. Wall, c.1751-83, Flight 1783-93, Flight & Barr, 1793-1807, Barr, Flight & Barr 1807-13, Flight, Barr & Barr, 1813-40, Kerr & Binns 1852-62, Royal Worcester Porcelain Co. Ltd., 1862 to present day.

Bibliography

Aslin, E.	*The Aesthetic Movement,* London, 1969
Barnard, J.	*Victorian Ceramic Tiles,* London, 1972
Bemrose, G.	*Nineteenth Century English Pottery & Porcelain* London, 1952
Blacker, J.F.	*19th Century English Ceramic Art,* London, n.d.
Brayshaw Gilhespy, F. & Budd, D.M.	*Royal Crown Derby China,* London, 1964
Eyles, D.	*Royal Doulton 1815-1965,* London, 1965
Godden, G.A.	*Encyclopaedia of British Pottery & Porcelain Marks,* London, 1964
Godden, G.A.	*An Illustrated Encylopaedia,* London, 1966
Godden, G.A.	*Coalport and Coalbrookdale Porcelains,* London, 1970
Godden, G.A.	*Ridgway Porcelains,* London, 1972
Godden, G.A.	*Minton Pottery and Porcelain of the First Period,* London, 1968
Godden, G.A.	*Victorian Porcelain,* London, 1970
Jewitt, L.	*Ceramic Art of Great Britain,* London, 1972
Lockett, T.A.	*Davenport Pottery and Porcelain,* London, 1972
Rice, D.G.	*Rockingham Pottery and Porcelain,* London, 1971
Sandon, H.	*Royal Worcester Porcelain,* London, 1973
Shinn, C. & D.	*Victorian Parian China,* London, 1971
Twitchett J.	*Royal Crown Derby* to be published by Barrie & Jenkins, 1975/6
Whiter, L.	*Spode – A History of the Family and Wares,* London, 1970

Museums

Most museums include small quantities of 19th century British porcelain amongst their exhibits but only one concentrates on the period — the Victoria and Albert Museum.

The Victoria and Albert also includes numerous pieces, as do Stoke-on-Trent museum and the Ironbridge museum. Many of the factories have already opened exhibits of their wares, the best being the Dyson Perrins Collection at Royal Worcester, others include the Minton/Royal Doulton at Stoke-on-Trent and the Coalport Showrooms which has examples of their early pieces.

Index to Illustrations

173, 174, 175, 176, 177, 195, 196, 252,
253, 254, 255, 256, 257, 258, 259, 260,
261, 262, 263, 278, 279, 280, 281, 282,
283, 312, 313, 345, 346, 347, 348, 349,
350, 441, 442, 443, 444, 445, 446, 447,
448, 449, 450, 451, 452, 453, 454, 455,
456, 457, 458, 459, 460, 461, 462, 463,
464, 465, 466, 467, 468, 469, 470, 471,
472, 473, 474, 475, 476, 477, 478, 479,
480, 481, 482, 483, 484, 495, 500

Unattributed   50, 123, 124, 125, 126, 150, 151, 152,
153, 178, 179, 180, 197, 198, 199, 200,
201, 202, 264, 265, 266, 284, 285, 286,
287, 288, 314, 485, 486, 487, 488